AF632237

A Critical Review of Writings in English

Ashutosh Dubey

ATLANTIC
PUBLISHERS & DISTRIBUTORS (P) LTD

Published by
ATLANTIC
PUBLISHERS & DISTRIBUTORS (P) LTD
7/22, Ansari Road, Darya Ganj, New Delhi-110002
Phones : +91-11-40775252, 23273880, 23275880, 23280451
Fax : +91-11-23285873
Web : www.atlanticbooks.com
E-mail : orders@atlanticbooks.com

Branch Office
5, Nallathambi Street, Wallajah Road, Chennai-600002
Phones : +91-44-64611085, 32413319
E-mail : chennai@atlanticbooks.com

Printed in India at Nice Printing Press, A-33/3A, Site-IV, Industrial Area, Sahibabad, Ghaziabad, U.P.

Dedicated to

My parents
(Late) Dr. Madan Mohan Dubey
and
Smt. Pushpalata Dubey

and my teachers

(Late) Dr. Surendra Singh Chandel
and
Dr. Smt. Usha Chandel

Preface

A Critical Review of Writings in English is an anthology of my critical essays, which mainly includes essays on some eminent Indian writers in English with reference to their respective works. Whereas I have tried to explore the generation clash in the world of Malgudi, so enchantingly created by R.K. Narayan, Girish Karnad's play *Bali* has also inspired me to make an attempt to analyse the thematic web of this multi-layered, though relatively less talked-about play. *The God of Small Things* has an intricate structural design that inspired me to have a closer look at it from this point of view. Jhumpa Lahiri's debut story collection *Interpreter of Maladies* does have many inviting facets to it and, therefore, apart from a critical appraisal of this book, there are two more essays separately on the immigrant experience and the portrayal of marital relationships in these stories. Manju Kapur's *Difficult Daughters* has earned for her a sound place in the firmament of Indian writers in English. Veermati, the protagonist in this novel, evokes a response that is repleted with uneasy questions and yet tries to view her with an understanding she duely deserves. This anthology also includes essays on two most outstanding bilingual poets—Arun Kolatkar and Dilip Chitre. Whereas Kolatkar in his *Jejuri* presents his own version of Indian wasteland; Chitre evinces a wide range of poetic endeavours from scathing ironies to exploration of deep spiritual experiences.

Exile is not the same experience with a woman as it is for a man. Novelists like Anita Desai, Bharati Mukherjee, Manju

Kapur, and Jhumpa Lahiri have portrayed their women characters in exile with remarkable power and poignancy. The essay "Images of Women in Exile" takes into account this aspect. Not much has been written on Satyajit Ray as a sci-fi writer. In one of the essays I have attempted to have a comparative look at him vis. the fictional writings of Jayant Vishnu Narlikar. This book has also an essay on the critical appraisal of the short stories of Krishna Baldev Vaid who has translated some of his writings into English from Hindi and is one of the most experimental writers. One of the essays analyses Meena Alexander's novel *Nampally Road*, whereas another one examines the emerging Indian urban youth in the novels of Chetan Bhagat.

Apart from these, this anthology includes essays on Tennessee Williams, Anne Tyler and Ibsen's *A Doll's House*. Also, two essays deal respectively with popular literature and the complex act of translation.

I am thankful to Atlantic Publishers and Distributors (P) Ltd., New Delhi, for bringing this book out with quality and taste. I hope it will be useful to the students and scholars of English.

Ashutosh Dubey

Contents

1

Generation Clash in Malgudi

Family signifies emotional security, moral support, domestic bliss and at the same time, it is also the stage for the continuous struggle and emotional conflict, the articulation of which remains a challenging task. The process of the yielding of the old order is never an easy one. It entails a lot of trials and tribulations. Generation clashes are inevitable as one generation that is firmly entrenched in its attitudes, lifestyle and values is challenged by the next one. The younger generation brings into question the wisdom of the older and the conflict ensues. Whereas the old generation dismisses it as irrelevant and worthless; it tries to carve a different path for itself which often gets disapproval of the old generation. In a typical Indian milieu, the generational clash assumes significant dimensions as at least three generations live under the same roof. This conflict is perennially staged in families causing a lot of mental and emotional strife and sometimes even culminates into the break-up of families.

Naturally, this offers a gripping and poignant drama to a novelist like R.K. Narayan who happens to be one of the greatest chroniclers of the oddities and absurdities of the people inhabiting this Malgudian world. This generation clash is presented in three of his novels: *The World of Nagraj*, *The Financial Expert* and *The Vendor of Sweets*. Narayan deals with this theme in his characteristics tragicomic manner but nevertheless he does so with great power and charm. His aim does not seem to suggest remedies as this clash defies simple solutions and easy-way outs. However, he charts the resultant turbulence and upheaval rivetingly.

In *The World of Nagraj* (1990), Tim, the son of the worldly wise brother of Nagraj—our good-for-nothing idler sort of protagonist, leaves the home of his father to live with his uncle. He has great affection for his nephew but it never occurs him to ask some necessary questions or guide him to the right pathways. By and large, he avoids confronting his nephew. When one evening Tim passes by him leaving a trail of alcoholic scent, he asks timidly about it and gets the answer that it is eau-de-cologne some chap sprayed on him. Obviously, Tim takes advantage of Nagraj's simplicity and goes about his ways unhindered. The age-old solution to put fetters of responsibility on such unbridled youths by marrying them off does not work as Tim with his wife joins a notorious club of Malgudi and refuses to leave it. Gopu disowns his son and returns to his village, whereas Nagraj resignedly watches the coming back of Tim and his wife to his home. Once again he asks no questions:

> He has come back in the same manner as he left—no explanation or any elaborate discussion—not in his nature, why should one expect anything different? I'll take him as he is. If his father wants him, he is welcome to come and take him, I am only a milestone. I stay and others come and pass. I must only watch, not ask questions. Tim's life and actions, as ever, a mystery. But God has not endowed me with a temperament to solve mysteries. I have to accept them, that's all....

Here, the placidity and tranquility of the complacent old world is disturbed by the vital, energetic but misguided and directionless new generation. Neither the stoicism of Nagraj nor the fierce resistance of Gopu supervenes and finally they both reconcile erratic ways of Tim.

Somewhat similar, but a more serious delineation of this conflict is seen in *The Financial Expert* (1967). Margayya starts his financial career sitting in the shade of a banyan tree, advising the people of Malgudi how to extract loans from the cooperative bank. He grows rich and becomes a financial wizard in course of time. His son Balu revolts against school and runs away. Though he is declared dead, Margayya does not give up and after a lot of efforts, brings him back to home. Balu proves to be the nemesis of Margayya. Spoilt and pampered, he under the evil influence of Dr. Pal, adopts evil ways and eventually Margayya loses his fortune. He becomes a chastened soul after having lost his money which plagued his relationship with the world. He advises his son to go to the banyan tree with a pen and an ink bottle and sit under it, just the way he had started his life. But the boy hesitates as to what people would think. At this Margayya resolves to do the same himself and is not at all perturbed ate the prospect of starting from the scratch. This journey back to square one is fraught with the lessons he has derived from his experiences. Completely relaxed, after this turmoil in his life he wants to play with his grandson. Experience is the best teacher and we hope that Balu will be a responsible person and mature person after having gone through the hardships of life. The confrontation of two worlds here is steeped in irony as Margayya after losing everything seem to have attained his equanimity whereas Balu appears to be as confused as ever:

> The boy stood ruminating. He was looking crushed: "How can I go and sit there? What will people think?" (218)

The generation clash is the main theme of *The Vendor of Sweets* (1967). Jagan is a prosperous widower, a sweet-vendor who shares an uneasy relationship with his son Mali. Mali loses his mother at an early age and does not reciprocate the affection shown to him by his father. He announces his decision to abandon school to go America to become a writer and comes back with a half-Korean, half-American wife and also with a bizarre scheme for marketing a novel-writing machine which further adds to Jagan's bewilderment. Later, he is shocked to know that Grace is not Mali's wife and yet they have been living together. His cherished notions of marriage and morals receive a great jolt. The estrangement between father and son reaches its Zenith as Jagan gives up this futile attempt to come to terms with the new world and seeks his freedom, renouncing his shop and going away; finally overcoming his weakness for his son:

> The cousin was amazed at the transformation in Jagan, who kept repeating, his eyes still wet, "A little prison life

> won't harm him anyone. I must not miss the eight-thirty bus at Market Gate...." (185)

Here, we can remember Margayya's transformation as well. When Balu seems undecided and wary of people's reaction at his starting from the scratch, Margayya says:

> Very well then, if you are not going, I am going on with it, as soon as I am able to leave this bed.... Now get the youngster here. I will play with him. Life has been too dull without him in this house. (217)

These three novels evince some similar patterns. Gopu, Jagan and Margayya—all three fathers are affluent. Gopu and Margayya's wives are self-effacing creatures whereas Jagan's wife is dead. They do not exercise influence on their sons or try to control them. Tim, Balu and Mali—all three sons abandon school as school symbolizes order and discipline and offers resistance to the unchecked freedom. There is an obvious communication gap between two generations. Jagan realizes—"He has grown up with me, under the same roof, but how little I have known him!" (35). His wife was the bridge between him and Mali and after she died, "the barrier had come into being. The boy had ceased to speak to him normally" (37). Jagan's affection goes unrequited. All three sons are headstrong, foolhardy, reckless and unconcerned about the sentiments and feeling of their parents. It is the breach between father and son that some sort of a mediating agent becomes necessary. Cousin in *The Vendors of Sweets*, Dr. Pal who turns villain towards the end in *The Financial Expert*, and the talkative man in *The World of Nagraj* are the people who are better informed about the youngsters than their fathers. Jagan can hardly communicate with Mali, Nagraj does not have the nerve to confront his nephew, whereas Gopu and Margayya resort to forceful resistance but fail.

This lack of communication and understanding seems to have stemmed from some psychological obstacle in case of Mali and Jagan; but it has no apparent reason in case of Tim-Gopu and Balu-Margayya. Perhaps, Narayan ironically implies that the worldly successful fathers fail miserably when it comes to matters of heart. They amass wealth and are prosperous in the materialistic sense, but they lose on their home front. Margayya believes: "Money alone is important in this world. Everything else will come to us naturally if we have money in our purse" (21). He has great hopes for his son but all these hopes are shattered as Balu spoils his life despite Margayya's efforts to salvage it. Jagan renounces resignedly and Gopu goes back to attend his farm. Money appears to be in the distancing agent which casts an ominous shadow on the relationship between these two generations.

The rebellion of the new generation in Malgudi ends in a fiasco as it is aimless and directionless from the beginning. There is no headway for Tim, Balu and Mali. In their bid to upset the established order, they have ruined their own lives. Mali is full of plans but these plans are extremely impractical and grandiose. After his brief stint in the ill-famous club 'Kismet', Tim is back in the house of Nagraj with no prospects for a better future. Balu, having tasted the fruits of prosperity, is unable to reconcile himself to his present adversity. They are on the same cross-roads in the end where they were at the beginning.

The old generation is not prepared to take on these unexpected and unpredictable twists and turns offered by the new generation. It is confused, puzzled and rather intimidated by the audacity of the new generation. The morals are thrown to the winds, the beliefs are questioned, the worldly-wisdom is ridiculed. The material success attained by Jagan, Margayya and Gopu is the fruit of hard work and perseverance. The younger generation having inherited this fortune, does not realize its true worth and let it go down the drains.

It seems that some sort of realization dawns on Jagan and Margayya. They both have attained the peace of mind—that equanimity which gives them strength for their future. In this way, their sons have taught them lessons of their lives. But the question remains: have these sons learnt anything from their own experiences? The generation clash leads the older generation to resign whereas the younger one seems as flabbergasted as ever. There is no headway, no progression; Narayan generally leaves such tales in an impasse.

The absence of proper dialogue, the inability to understand the point of view of each other, the unknown apprehensions and psychological barriers, the lack of a common platform, the chinks in the emotional bond and sometimes the inexplicable hostility are some of the traits of this generation clash. The older generation's notions of the well-being of the younger generation are mocked at, the plans are foiled, and pressure evokes resistance and culminates into clash. Narayan sometimes also hints at the inherent yet inexplicable element in the relationship of two generations which simply refuses to forge any kind of mutual understanding. It gnaws into its vitals and contributes to complete estrangement. Any logical explanation of it is quite difficult and the resolution of the problem rules out the simplification of all sorts. Narayan tries to capture exactly this phenomenon with all its enigmatic and baffling facets.

In the generation clash, as it takes place in Malgudi, neither of the side emerges victorious. It leads to that tragicomic sense of waste the evocation of which is perhaps aimed by the novelist. As has been stated above, R.K. Narayan does not resort to simple solutions. He may be sympathizing with the older generation, yet a destitute Balu and an imprisoned Mali also call for a sympathetic approach. The complex contours of this clash are presented before us in all dimensions. Generation clash is a universally significant theme and Narayan with his uncanny grasp over Indian milieu records its nuances to the best of his creative powers.

REFERENCES

Narayan, R.K. (1990). *The World of Nagraj*, Mysore: Indian Thought Publications.

——. (1967). *The Vendor of Sweets*, Mysore: Indian Thought Publications, rep. 1997.

——. (1958). *The Financial Expert*, Mysore: Indian Thought Publications, rep. 1996.

2

The Thematic Web in Girish Karnad's *Bali: The Sacrifice*

Memories slide
meld and fuse.
Discreet moments
get flung together
strung in a single moment.
Then the moment
Distends, spreads
into years.[1]

Girish Karnad's play—*Bali: The Sacrifice* draws upon the thirteenth-century Kannada epic *Yashodhara Charita* by Janna which is linked to an eleventh-century Sanskrit epic *Yashtilaka* by Somdeva Suri. The play has a complex thematic web entailing the themes of conflict between violence represented by the sacrificial rites and non-violence, fidelity and betrayal, conversion of faith and the pull of entrenched *samskaras*, and guilt and forgiveness. This layered edifice of the play gets intensified by the twists and turns in the relationships of its four major characters. Two of the them are males—the King and the Mahout, and two females—the Queen and the Queen Mother who are respectively wife and mother of the King. Like a typical Indian son and husband, the King is caught between his wife and mother who are openly hostile to each other. Their opposite attitudes towards sacrificial rites is one prominent cause of this hostility—yet we discern that they have a mutual dislike and a lack of trust remains on both sides.

While a young lad, the King impresses his young betrothed with the boasts that he can easily hunt lions and placates his miffed would-be wife by showing her "how to knock a bird off a branch" even without a catapult. Initially thrilled at this boastful claim, the Queen is revolted when she actually finds the bird dead and the prince is contrite, witnessing her grief. The King converts to the faith of his wife, becomes a Jain much against the wish of his mother who seems to have a penchant for talking 'daggers'. Caught between these two strong, inflexible women, the King emerges as an understanding and adjusting male who does not wish to offend either of them but who has to take a definite stand on issues. We also find that he has been quite successful in curbing the instinct of violence to a great extent, so much so that he let's go mahout scot-free even in the face of his grave offence of defiling his Queen. He is a kind of interpreter between these two women who do not understand each other's language, intentions and sentiments—a daunting task doomed to failure. He has shown great flexibility and openness of mind in his embracing Jainism even in the teeth of his mother's opposition. His unwillingness to forgive his wife even after her act of infidelity incurs the wrath of his mother to such an extent that she calls him 'impotent' and spits on his face. He puts up with all this and more. Though he converts to Jainism, his '*samskaras*' compels him to sacrifice a cock made of dough to avert the evil consequences of the Queen's infidelity. His struggle to transform himself and his very human lapses while doing so make him quite vulnerable.

The Queen is unflinching in her faith. Ironically, her relationship with the King ensues with violence. The killing of the bird falls like a shadow on their conjugal life. She is assertive and convincing enough to snatch away the King from his mother and brings about his conversion. She loves her "affectionate, gentle, trusting" husband but is unable to resist the spell of the voice of the Mahout that leads to their physical union. What is extraordinary is her attitude. She does not repent nor does she feel any guilt or remorse. Her refusal to join the King in the symbolic sacrifice of the clay-bird is not so much an act of repugnance for even intentional violence as it is her protest against her damnation as an adulterous. She shows an uncanny insight into the psyche of Mahout who seems to be a victim of inferiority complex due to his ugliness and low caste.

Queen: You're not ugly, you know. You are lonely.

Mahout (defensive): I live alone, if that's what you mean. That's all right by me.

Queen: That's why you are holding me prisoner. You don't want to know my name. You want someone to talk to. (81)

It is not that there exists some invisible breach between the King and the Queen. She does not allow Mahout to speak against her husband about whose identity he is unaware. When he suggests that she has come to him because her husband cannot satisfy her physically, she refutes it there and then. Her surrender to Mahout is enigmatic and one can only attribute it to the sensuous singing of Mahout who is conscious of this kind of charm of his voice and is not ready to exchange it for a handsome face. The Queen is unwavering in her resolve to stick to her creed of non-violence in spite of what has transpired between her and Mahout. Unyielding and unrelenting, the Queen sticks to her ground against the sacrificial rites and stops the Queen Mother from sacrificing animals in order to celebrate her pregnancy. Animal slaughter is indeed an act of violence; but so is the slaying of faith, loyalty and fidelity without which the marital bond crumbles—isn't the Queen guilty of that violence? Violating the code of marital conduct she probably can ill-afford to be so righteous in her stand against sacrificial rites. If the Queen Mother seeks to placate her gods through animal sacrifices; the Queen sacrifices the trust reposed in her by her husband in her sensuous swoon and though she assures the King that she won't do it ever again, she has no pangs of conscience for what has been transpired between her and the Mahout.

Queen Mother is a loving mother who has to beat an inevitable retreat in this tug-of-war with her daughter-in-law. There is an obvious and mutual lack of trust between them. Queen Mother is a traditional upholder of the patriarchal values of Indian society where the greatest obligation of a married woman is to beget a son and it becomes all the more imperative if the woman happens to be the Queen. Her daughter-in-law has disappointed her in the matter of the royal heir. Queen

Mother uses her tongue as a whiplash, her speech is fiery and laced with violence:

> Queen Mother: I should cut her to pieces…feed her to the wolves and vultures. Do it, son, now!
>
> King: Don't be hysterical, Mother—
>
> Queen Mother: Throw her bones to the dogs. She has betrayed you. You are not bound by your vows now. All this nonsense about non-violence. It had to go. Kill the harlot and her lover. If you won't do it, I'll do it. Let me fetch my sacrificial knife from the temple. I'll…. (107)

Her relationship with the Queen has all the usual strife intrinsic in a typical relationship between mother-in-law and daughter-in-law; it gets more tangled because of their diametrically opposite stands, viz. violence versus non-violence. However stringent she is with her daughter-in-law, she is a fond mother who loves her son deeply. She has an uncanny insight into the mind of her son and is so perceptive that she senses the infidelity of the Queen only through the reaction and the physical signs of distress caused by it on the King. Though she is unflinching in her faith, she relents for the sake of her son's happiness: "Do you think I like torturing you—my only child, the light of my life?" (108).

Mahout imparts another thematic twist to this play. He is a low-caste who has the gift of a heavenly voice. It is a voice that can seduce the Queen. His rough, uncouth ways of behaviour charm the Queen in a strange manner. He is ugly and has a complex about his looks, but he is aware of the sensuous appeal of his voice. He is full of suppressed rage for being discriminated against because of his 'low-caste'. Says he: "People mock at Mahouts. Call us 'low-born'. But where would all your princes and kings be without us; I want to know. What would happen to their elephants? No elephants. No army. No pomp and splendour. No processions. No kings! Ha!" (80). Mahout is no martyr. To save his skin, he lies, pretends and can change colours swifter than a chameleon. Hatred has bred in him a seething anger that vents itself whenever it finds a place. Yet, he has his moments of self-esteem. When the Queen wants to give him her necklace, trying to seek his help in getting away from the ruined temple, he is irritated: "Keep it. If I'd wanted that bauble, I wouldn't have waited so long. That's your estimate of every lower caste man, isn't it? He's a good lay and all he wants is a piece of gold. I am an elephant-keeper, madam, not a fence, selling stolen jewelry" (84). Caught into this royal tangle, he employs every possible means to get out of this. His greatest concern is his voice and he suspects that through some religious ritual, he is going to be deprived of it. The Queen assures him that she won't let it happen to him. When the King turns his face away in disgust at this, the Queen says: "Spare me your disgust. You take your blood and gore. I'll choose his voice—" (105).

The Queen loves the King and yet has no compunction for her surrender to Mahout. The King is torn between his obligation towards his mother and love for the Queen. The Queen Mother is caught between her religious faith and her affection for her son. Mahout is proud of his hypnotic voice and yet a victim of inferiority complex due to the social strata he belongs. Thrilled at the sensuous spell his voice cast on the Queen, he is mortally terrified by its consequences. All the four characters of the play find themselves on the horns of some dilemma. It is here that *Bali: The Sacrifice* becomes a play with a complex thematic structure. Is it possible for a devoted wife to succumb to an ugly commoner's irresistible voice leading to infidelity? Can the religious fanaticism drive a mother to the extent of saying: "The only relationship in the world which does not wither and fade away is that of hate. That'll keep us together—at least so long as my son remains a Jain" (115). Can love and betrayal be so close together? The King is appalled and dismayed by the Queen's act but even this jolt does not make him judgmental. Repelled by this 'aberration' of his wife, he is still willing to have her 'back'. He has been successfully keeping his mother away from deciding things against his wife. The Queen has no regrets as she recounts:

> I was sleeping by your side. His singing woke me up. The song was so—don't know how to describe it. But suddenly the notes caressed me, enveloped me. They carried me away. For a brief moment, nothing mattered. The Palace,

> Me. You. Only the song. I felt like a flame burning bright. Pure. when I came to my senses, I was here. By his side. That's all there is to it. It just happensd.(Pause.) and what happened was beautiful.... I want to come back to you. I feel fuller. Richer. Warmer. But not ashamed. Because I didn't plan it. It happened. And it was beautiful. (119)

With its shocking end, *Bali: The Sacrifice* leaves us stunned. The Queen does not want to blot out the 'moment' with Mahout. She is not willing to perform even the symbolic sacrificial act to purge away her 'sin' and to avert the feared wrath of gods. When the King urges her to place her right hand on the back of his fist so he may push the blade into the cock-shaped lump of dough, she denies, calling it an act of violence. The King argues that there is no bloodshed. The Queen says: "Then why are you doing it? Why? Blood at least make sense if you believe in bloodthirsty gods. But this.... You can't knowingly fool yourself" (111). Just when the King plunges the sword into the cock, it begins to crow revealing the hideousness of even the symbolic act of violence. To prove it is made of dough, the King squashes it into a mass. Enraged, the Queen picks up the sword and lunges at the King to stab him. Then she realizes the extent of contamination of violence that has not even spared herself and presses the point of the blade on her womb and impales herself on the sword. Thus, a champion of the cause of non-violence meets her ironically violent end. Thematically layered, the play culminates into a moment of realization for all its characters.

NOTE

1. Girish Karnad. *Two Plays by Girish Karnad, The Dreams of Tipu Sultan and Bali: The Sacrifice*. New Delhi, Oxford University Press, 2004, p. 93. Print. Subsequent references to this work have been incorporated in the text itself after quotes.

3

The Architectonics of *The God of Small Things*

> The great stories are the ones you have heard and want to hear again. The ones you can enter anywhere and inhabit comfortably. They don't deceive you with thrills and trick-endings. They don't surprise you with the unforeseen. They are as familiar as the house you live in or the smell of your lover's skin. You know how they end, yet you listen as though you don't.... That is their mystery and their magic.[1]

It may be debatable whether in her debut novel *The God of Small Things*, Arundhati Roy tells us a great story, yet the manner in which she tells it is indeed that of a great story. She tells her story within the first few pages and yet revives the innocence of the reader so that he willingly becomes interested in 'how' and 'why' instead of 'what'. An architect by her education, Arundhati designs this intricately balanced structure with a careful arrangement of graphics and designs. The beginning contains the end and the narrative unfolds towards it. Sophie Mol's funeral is described at the very outset. She actually arrives in Aymenem in the chapter sixth, 132 pages later. Her tragedy takes place in the chapter sixteenth. And as Propertius said, "The shade of the dead escapes from the funeral pyre and returns to our midst"—not only Sophie Mol but the dead past itself grows robust and alive—waiting to pounce on the living ones.

Arundhati has admitted that she had not written the first chapter first.[2] Inspired by Kathakali dance—the narrative dispenses with a linear structure in favour of a cyclical one.

Its complex patterning makes it meander through several time frames. Each small movement in the book is refracted through the lenses of the past and future, making precious even the most ordinary events. All this 'arrangement' at times baffles even writers like Nayantara Sehgal who could not "understand whether we were in the past or present."[3] To her, all these 'capital letters and repetitions' are to blame for this so-called lack of communication.

That brings us to the linguistic structure of this novel. In fact, here language, the narrative and the structure are so melded together that characters, events, places refuse to shine in isolation. It is with a poet's minuteness and vision that Arundhati Roy invents an almost code-language, suffused with cross-references. The narrative is resonant of echoes—echoes of feelings—that are signified by certain expressions. Thus, Estha becomes pointy shoes and a spoiled puff; a fountain in Love-in-Tokyo signifies Rahel, a mortgaged glass eye replaces Vellya Paapen, a read-aloud voice substitutes Chacko, a pair of slanted sun glasses and a violin represent Mammachi, a moth embodies Pappachi's spirit, a brown leaf on a black back becomes an image for Velutha. In this process, the novel invents the language in which it is written. The poetic device of refrain or rather that of repetend provides unifying threads of the story and reinforces emotion and meaning. The repetition of lines, even seemingly non-sensical phrases is incantatory or sepulchral. The idiom of the narrative structure discovers itself in verbal combinations (stoppited), amusing coinages (aftermare), turning adjectives into nouns (One Loved a Little Less), running words together (whatisit ?) or breaking them (Lay. Ter or prer Nun sea ayshun), fashioning verbs (furry-whirring, sariflapping) and creative distortion of words (infinnate, dus to dus), etc.

Arundhati Roy exploits the creative extendibility of linguistic code, using unorthodox spellings to suggest a character's accent. For such purposes, she also makes use of graphological devices of spelling, punctuation and capitalization as well as lexical repetitions of various kinds. She resorts to intra-associative meanings of simile and metaphor mingling tactile, auditory and kinesthetic vocabulary. One area of sensation is translated into and invigorated by another, the whole effect being supercharged by grammatical and lexical repetition. To record the imprint of living experience, she turns to analogical language of simile and metaphor:

> Heaven opened and the water hammered down, reviving the reluctant old well, green mossing the pigless pigsty, carpet bombing still, tea-coloured puddles the way memory bombs still, tea-coloured minds. The grass looked wet green and pleased. Happy earthworms frolicked purple in the slush. Green nettles nodded. Trees bent. (10)
>
> With every monsoon, the old car settled more firmly into the ground like an angular, arthritic hen settling stiffly on her clutch of eggs, with no intention of ever getting up. Grass grew around its flat tyres. The Paradise Pickles & Preserves signboard rotted and fell inwards like a collapsed crown.
>
> A creeper stole a look at itself in the remaining mottled half of the cracked driver's mirror.
>
> A sparrow lay dead on the back seat. She had found her way through a hole in the windscreen. Tempted by some seat sponge for her nest. She never found her way out. No one noticed her panicked car-window appeals. She died on the back seat, with her legs in the air. Like a joke. (296)

The playful linguistic design is no mere embellishment—it is an ambitious endeavour to turn language itself into fiction. In *The God of Small Things*, language is the narrator, made of the stuff smells and colours are made of; evoking that pristine innocence when we used to imbibe impressions of the world with a fine set of antennae radiating from every pore of our consciousness. The interrelated movements of the narrative, based on the structural repetitions, create Arundhati's fictional ontology. The intrinsic, invoking power of this sign-language has been able to achieve the paradoxical feat of making the narrative structure centripetal and centrifugal at the same time. Significantly, the novel ends with the word 'tomorrow'—defying the structural end itself, as the novel so inextricably entrenched in its language cannot afford to have an 'end'.

Thematically, the cross-currents of love and terror, and history and biology are presented in the course of the narrative on principles of harmony and contrast. The story of a forbidden, cross-caste love and the inhuman extents to which a community would go in order to protect its 'structure', ambushes a different story of transgression. Architect Arundhati builds two houses on either side of the river—the Aymenem House and the History House. The Aymenem House is cluttered with broken dreams like Chacko's 'pickle Baron Dreams', Baby Kochamma's escape into the crazy world of television, Ammu's aborted attempt to get away from the house, her doomed return and her final exile. Here Estha and Rahel as children watch and understand the happenings and lose their sense of self-preservation; as adults, in an attempt to transgress, they break the love laws and share hideous grief together. It is a house around which the loss of Sophie Mol steps softly and ushers Estha and Rahel through childhood into adulthood.

On the other side of the river, waiting for Estha and Rahel is the History House where an old Englishman ghost, sickled to a tree, was abrogated by a pair of two-egg twins. In a variety of ways, the History House is the nemesis of Aymenem House. The needs of Chacko and Ammu may be of a different nature, yet in the Aymenem House there is a separate entrance through which 'objects' of Chacko's 'Needs' enter and in the History House, the object of Ammu's needs meets his tortured end. In between these two houses flows the river Meenanchal where history slips away and biology takes over. Meenanchal takes its due in the form of Sophie Mol—a tragedy whose shadow looms large on the narrative.

Between the House and the river lies the family business—Paradise Pickles and Preserves. The pickle business is an ironical metaphor for a novel in which the past is pickled and preserved in the smells, colours and the 'captured and redreamed dreams'.

Though the novel has been written in third person, mostly, it has been seen through the eyes of Estha and Rahel. The linguistic splendor, by and large, owes itself to their observation, experience and understanding as children. Estha and Rahel are 'reflectors', 'centers of consciousness' through whom Arundhati Roy filters her narrative. These reflectors are rather turbid, sense-bound 'camera-eyes' adding intensities of their own:

> In these early amorphous years when memory had only just begun, when life was full of beginnings and no ends, and everything was for ever, Esthappen and Rahel thought of themselves together as Me, and separately, individually, as We or Us. As though they were a rare breed of Siamese twins, physically separate, but with joint identities. Now these years later, Rahel has a memory of waking up one night giggling at Estha's funny dream. (2)

However, Arundhati varies the fictional point of view, claiming authorial omniscience, sometimes focusing on one character, sometimes giving us another character's version. Thanks to Arundhati's almost ubiquitous sardonic or irreverent tone, this shift remains imperceptible. Her essential sculpturesque genius, no doubt, allows for the tonal variations that range from a generous use of *lingua franca* to the most solemn poetic intensity.

The oppositional structures, as manifested in the Aymenem House and the History House can also be seen in the way Arundhati develops her characters. There are two groups of characters in the novel. The first abides by the old social structure whereas another group makes a total transition from the values of the first group to the 'anti-values' of itself. The first group believes in the blind adherence while the second group tries to break free from a social order which is suffocating. Baby Kochamma, Mammachi, Vellya Paapen, Chacko, etc. belong to the first group; whereas Ammu, Velutha, Estha and Rahel move from 'adherence' to 'transgression'. Both these groups pay the price for what they choose. Baby Kochamma's abandoned 'ornamental' garden is a symbol of the stagnation and rot which is the inevitable outcome of being 'static'. Ammu-Velutha and Estha-Rahel violate the social order, stick to the small things and reject the big things. Velutha dies and it is not death for the rest of them 'Just the end of the living' (321).

It is Ammu's abandonment of the values represented by the first group that shapes the plot of this novel. At first, she appears one of them—a snob, over-fastidious and righteous mother, fussy about cleanliness and obsessed about the children making the right impressions, and correcting them every so often:

> Rahel was frightened by the way Ammu said CLEAN and DIRTY so loudly. (150)
>
> When you disobey me in the public, everybody gets the wrong impression. (149)
>
> If I am talking to somebody, you may interrupt me only if it is very urgent. When you do, please say "Excuse me". I will punish you very severely if you disobey these instructions. Please complete your corrections. (159)

But in the heart of her hearts—"Ammu felt that she would die, wither and die—...if she had to endure another minute of Chako's proud, tennis-trophy smile. Or the undercurrent of sexual jealousy that emanated from Mammachi or Baby Kochamma's conversation..." and she 'aches' for Velutha "with the whole of her biology" (330) which leads to Baby Kochamma's remark: "How could she stand the smell? Haven't you noticed, they have a particular smell, these paravans?" (78). But this is not just biology, it is the 'Unsafe Edge' in Ammu that make her publicly admit to her relationship with Velutha. This moral development of Ammu's character involves the passage from one side to the other, and represents one of the distinguishing structural features of *The God of Small Things*.

In her fictional rendering, Arundhati Roy, above all, emerges as an artist who blends psychological sequencing with presentational sequencing and creates, in the process, her jigsaw puzzle of a tale that invites the reader for the teasing and pleasing task to piece it together. Very much like Rahel who happens to be a student of Architecture, Arundhati also has a *sui generis* plan to build-up her tale and probably again like Rahel, she remains indifferent to the passionate critiques.

NOTES

1. Arundhati Roy, *The God of Small Things*. New Delhi: India Ink, 1997, p. 229. All the quotations from the novel are from this edition.
2. In an interview with Urvashi Butalia. *Outlook*, April 9, 1997, p. 73.
3. Quoted in "English, chutneyfied", Sagrika Ghosh. *Outlook*, Oct. 27, 1997, p. 125.

4

Jhumpa Lahiri's *Interpreter of Maladies*—A Study

Jhumpa Lahiri belongs to the second-generation Indian-American and her debut collection of nine stories—*Interpreter of Maladies* has made a deep mark on the present scenario of Indian English writing. The Pulitzer winning collection has underlined the promise and potential of a significant writer. Born in London in 1967 and raised in Rhodes Island, Jhumpa Lahiri is the daughter of Bengali parents. Her heritage and culture are influenced by both India and United States. She records the emotional voyages of characters seeking love beyond the barriers of nations, cultures, religions and generations. Imbued with the immigrant sensibility, these stories speak with universal eloquence and compassion to everyone who has ever felt like an outsider. They chart the experiences of both first and second generation Indian immigrants, presenting the old world (India) bumping against the new (America). Against the backdrop of culture clash, the stories in this collection deal with the universal lessons in love, individual's struggle to overcome the change, insecurities within relationships which are at time withering and at time prove to be unshakable, ancient traditions of ancestors and the baffling prospects of the new world, maladies sometimes properly diagnosed and even cured, at other times misinterpreted, matters which seem temporary and yet affect the whole life, unexpectedly cruelty and gradual understanding, the psychic mechanisms to resist the environment and the power of survival. These are the major themes around which Jhumpa weaves her tales.

The title story of this collection has been chosen for both the O'Henry Award and the annual Best American short stories. It is set in Puri and tells of an encounter between an affluent American couple who along with their children is tracing their Indian heritage and their Indian guide—Mr. Kapasi. The story operates at several levels of meaning. It is about the complexities of communication, understanding, interpretation and finally—disillusionment. Mina Das, the tourist wife and Mr. Kapasi, the guide have one thing in common—their loveless faltering marriage. Mr. Kapasi is perked up by her interest in him and begins to fantasize a romantic relationship with her. When she describes his job—as an interpreter in a doctor's clinic translating Guajarati spoken by some of his parents, as 'romantic', he is mildly intoxicated. At the crisis-point of the story, Mina confesses a secret to Mr. Kapasi—a secret which is malady afflicting her for the past eight years. She tells him that one of the couple's two sons was actually fathered by her husband's Punjabi-Indian friend during a brief visit. This is the malady which she hopes Mr. Kapasi will provide a remedy for, because he has been an interpreter of maladies. But then Mrs. Das does not resemble the patients in the doctor's office and Mr. Kapasi does not know what to say. All he could say is "Is it really pain your feel, Mrs. Das, or is it guilt?" And the rapport, which had begun to form between them, instantly evaporates. Both feel disillusioned and deceived. He is betrayed by his belief in their cultural affinity, she by misplaced faith in his ability to understand her.

This impervious nature of communication is, once again, at the centre of the story "A Temporary Matter". It is the tale of a dying marital relationship over which is hovering the common grief caused by their stillborn baby. During this phase when they are avoiding each other, for five days their electricity is cut off for an hour. That reminds the wife of India where the current disappears for hours at a stretch. During these power failures at her grandmother's house, in her childhood, they all had to say something—a little poem, a joke, a fact about the world. This childhood story is revived at the wife's insistence that, in the dark, they should say something to each other they have never told before. A strange, bittersweet game ensues amid the detritus of their life together. Darkness becomes quite revealing in which they try to discover the real malady that is afflicting their relationship. The story is remarkable for its quietude and submerged pain. It is also one of the significant features of Jhumpa Lahiri's stories that the central situation moves towards a certain moment of knowledge which illumines the whole story. This moment of knowledge acts like a prism through which the story can be seen in its various hues. "A Temporary Matter" ends with the sentence: "They wept together, for the things they now knew" (22). In "Interpreter of Maladies", Mina Das realizes that her expectations from Mr. Kapasi are ill-conceived:

> She turned to him and glared, mustard oil thick on her frosty pink lips. She opened her mouth to say something, but as she glared at Mr. Kapasi some certain knowledge seemed to pass before her eyes, and she stopped. It crushed him, he knew at that moment that he was not even important enough to be properly insulted. (66)

In the story "Sexy", Miranda realizes the futility of her relationship with a married Indian only when a seven year old Indian boy interprets the meaning of the word 'Sexy'—a compliment paid to her by lover—as 'loving someone you don't know'. Miranda feels "Rohini's words under her skin the same way she'd felt Dev's. But instead of going hot, she felt numb". (109). It snaps something in her and she comes to her senses. "The Blessed House" is also about the gradual realization of the incompatibility of the couple. The husband gives in against the tenacity of his wife's whims. We wonder how long the beauty and charm of the wife will keep up the marriage from falling apart. It may turn out to be, after all, just a temporary matter—but then one can never be sure in Lahiri's stories as they defy predictability. All these stories feature marriages that have been betrayed, rushed into, invaded and exhausted. Still, they are not about disappointment; they manifest a hunger to know, to discover more of the other person, and knowledge slowly but surely—it helps to communicate.

Stories like "Mrs. Sen's", "The Third and Final Continent" and "When Mr. Pirzada came to Dine" chart the immigrant experience from various angles. In "The Third and Final Continent", the protagonist develops a taste, patiently and painstakingly, not only for American cornflakes but also for American life. On a different level, the story also records his relationship with his American landlady of over a hundred year's age. At first unnerved by her calcified habits, he gradually develops an understanding of her that draws out his tenderness. Ironically, it is her approval of the protagonist's wife as a 'perfect lady' that actually breaks the ice between the couple and they arrive at last. He is grief-stricken at the death of this lady of exceptional grit and independence and says: "Mrs. Croft's was the first death I mourned in America, for hers was the first life I had admired" (196). But towards the end there is a sense of uneasiness in him as the old ways of life are coming under threat and he is not sure whether his son will continue to speak Bengali or eat rice with his hands—"things we sometimes worry he will no longer do after we die" (197). Needless to say, this is one of the major concerns of the Indian immigrants who helplessly watch their children losing the sense of belonging.

The title character in the story "Mrs. Sen's" is diametric opposite of the protagonist in "The Third and Final Continent". Born in India, she still dresses in saris, applies vermilion on her forehead and seeks escape in memory for self-preservation. Caretaker of an American boy Eliot, she represents those Indian immigrants who find themselves stranded in a country and a culture that is not their own but which demands conformity from them. Mrs. Sen's stubborn refusal and reluctance to learn driving seems to be a psychic device of her own kind of resistance to this dictate of conformity from the new world. Looking at the traffic, her English falters and she, with a sense of bewilderment, says to Eliot: "Everyone, this people, too much in their world." Ironically again, this is true of herself also as she wistful declares: 'Everything is there' (that is, in India) and her tragedy lies in the fact that she herself no longer is. Seeking refuge in memory, she keeps listening to the tape in which the voices of her relatives are recorded. Same is the case with Mr. Pirzada, who, in the story "When Mr. Pirzada came to Dine" also relieves the past by putting a pocket-watch on the coffee-table before dinner. This pocket-watch is set according to the time in Dacca to which he belongs. The loss of familiar and the ingenious devices these immigrants invent to cope with an alien world is conveyed with touching sensitivity and compassion in these stories.

Stories like "A Real Durwan" and "The Cure of Bibi Haldar" lack the brilliance and even verisimilitude to a certain extent. Anecdotal in nature, they are sketches of subaltern personalities and betray a bit patronizing gaze of a visiting non-resident. However, touching these stories are in parts, on the whole, they remain pedestrians in comparison to other stories of the collection where Jhumpa Lahiri very deftly deals with the intercultural miscommunications or emerges as a capable interpreter of the emotional pain and suffering of her characters.

Deceptively understated, unobtrusive and elegant, Lahiri's prose is conspicuously free from Indianisms which generally clutter up Indian English. There are no stylistic acrobatics and no linguistic innovations. She spares with metaphor and does not resort to the use of poetic language for effect. She has patience and love for details and her descriptions, especially of women's clothing are delightful. Her situations may be uncanny but they never lack probability. She chisels her stories through concrete details and implied emotion and her peculiar touch crystallizes the ways in which human affections encounter the cultural forms that threaten to circumscribe them. Her characters always emerge finely etched—revealing themselves gradually in the context of the central situation. She uses the subtle brush strokes of words to bring out the nuances in relationships as well as behavioural patterns of individuals. An example can be cited from "The Third and Final Continent" where the narrator, rather than leave his weekly rent on the piano, hands it to Mrs. Croft—his fierce and independent American landlady. The narrator says:

> The night when I came home, she did not slap the bench, but out of habit I sat beside has an usual. She asked me if I had checked the lock, but she mentioned nothing about the flag on the moon.

Instead she said:

"It was kind of you!"

"I beg your pardon, madam?"

"Very kind of you!"

She was still holding the envelope in her hands. (184)

The difference that is brought about by these small acts of kindness, courtesy, concern and compassion is expressed through the fewest possible words. It is also remarkable that the writer is successful especially in those stories where she sees through the eyes of a child—Eliot in "Mrs. Sen's", Rohini in "Sexy" and Lilia in "When Mr. Pirzada came to Dine" are the reflectors through which Jhumpa Lahiri filters her narrative. Probably, it is due to the fact that child is a peripheral character—not yet entirely absorbed into the manipulations and machinations of the adult world. The juvenile point of view lends a distinct colour to these stories.

Lahiri's depiction of Indian culture is not exaggerated or overbearing. These stories are replete with details of Indian names, food, cooking and wardrobe, which give a distinct flavour to them. It can also be interpreted as a device for the reassurance of the familiar into unfamiliar setting. With the increasing number of Indian immigrants, the presence of a growing market that laps up the exotic transformation of native realities cannot be denied. While catering to this need to a certain extent, the expatriate writing is also exploring the astonishing complexities of the diasporic life. With this precocious debut, Jhumpa Lahiri has excited great expectations. One can hope that she would delve deep into the world of second-generation-Indian Americans who are not struggling merely to be comfortable. *Interpreter of Maladies* is an ample justification for believing that she will continue to live up to these expectations.

REFERENCE

Lahiri, Jhumpa. *An Interpreter of Maladies* (New Delhi: HarperCollins Publishers India Pvt. Ltd., 1999), p. 22. Subsequent references to this book have been incorporated in the text itself after quotes.

5

Images of Marriage in Jhumpa Lahiri's *Interpreter of Maladies*

Marry, and with luck
it may go well
But when a marriage fails
Those who marry live at home in hell

—Euripides, *Orestes*

In diasporic writings, the images of home, family and marriage connote the attempts to rebuild home (away from original home) and therefore exert a powerful pull on the imagination of the writers of Indian diaspora. It is all the more significant when, like Jhumpa Lahiri, the writer happens to be brought up in the West and for whom the place called home is northwestern United States. Not surprisingly, her characters share a similar biography—they are entirely of the West with parents born and raised in India. The feminist consciousness is not much pronounced in Jhumpa Lahiri, especially where she delineates a marital relation belonging to her generation. Shobha in "A Temporary Matter" and Twinkle in "The Blessed House" have their say and their identity but Mrs. Sen in "Mrs. Sen's" and Mala in "The Third and Final Continent" belong to the first-generation Indian women immigrants who try their best to mould themselves according to the benevolent dictatorship of their husbands and the demands of a new world. However, Jhumpa's commitment is not to the feminist ideal, she seems to advocate a marital relation based on mutual understanding and respect. Her stress is on the individual's struggle to overcome change and insecurities within relationships.

Shobha and Shukumar in "A Temporary Matter" are suffering from the silence creeping into their relationship. Shukumar is troubled by images of parenthood as he is still a student at thirty-five. Their baby is born dead and this grief hovers over strained relations. Shukumar speaks to her with effort and gives up trying to amuse her. He is learning not to "mind the silences".[1] It is during this phase that for five days their electricity is cut off for an hour. This temporary matter of the power cut reminds Shobha of India where the current disappears for hours at a stretch and in order to pass the time, at her grandmother's house everybody had to say something. This childhood story is revived at her insistence that they should tell each other something they have never told before. Thus, they indulge in this bitter-sweet exchange of confessions amid the detritus of their life together and silence begins to thaw. They are able to talk to each other again, the forgotten warmth of the past is revived; but there are no simple solutions and Shobha announces her decision to shift to another apartment as she needs 'sometime alone'. The last confession of Shukumar is that he has held the body of his baby boy and he had promised himself that he would never tell Shobha about it, because he still loved her than it was one thing in her life that she had wanted to be a surprise. The story ends with Shobha turning the lights off, coming back to the table and sitting down with Shukumar joining her and "they wept together, for the things they now knew" (22). The story is steeped in understated, submerged pain emanating from the emotional confusion of the couple. The American lifestyle of the couple is set off their fascination for the rituals of the original country. "Their baby would never have a rice ceremony, even though Shobha had already made the guest list and decided on which of her three brothers she was going to ask to feed the child its first taste of solid food, at six months if it was a boy, seven if it was a girl" (11). The wife's moorings in Indian tradition and culture are contrasted with the husband, who has not spent much time in India and wishes now that he had "his own childhood story of India" (12). The disparity between the cultural backgrounds is merely hinted at, but it provides a clue to understand their respective emotional constitutions. Also, the predictability and ennui that creep into a stagnant relationship is suggested with a touch of humour. "My wife gave me a sweater-vest for my anniversary," he complained to the bartender, his head heavy with cognac. "What do you expect?" the bartender had replied. "You are married" (18).

Whatever is driving the marriage of Shobha and Shukumar on the rocks—one thing is sure—they have been faithful to each other. This can hardly be claimed for Mr. and Mrs. Das—an Indian-American couple, both born and raised in America, presently on the tour of India in "Interpreter of Maladies". Their guide is Mr. Kapasi who has been assisting a doctor, interpreting what the patients say in Gujarati. The marital relationships of Mr. and Mrs. Das and Mr. and Mrs. Kapasi are very much similar. When Mr. Kapasi looks at Das family, it seem to him that "they were in charge of the children only for one day; it was hard to believe they were regularly responsible for anything other than themselves" (49). He wonders whether Mr. and Mrs. Das are a bad match, just as he and his wife are. Their marriage is suffering from the bickering, the indifference, the protracted silences to which he has resigned himself. When Mr. Das takes unusual interest in his vocation as interpreter of maladies, he is mildly intoxicated and begins to dream of a 'romantic' relationship with her. But Mina Das wants him to interpret her malady—a secret that is troubling her for the past eight years—one of her sons is fathered by a friend of her husband. The story ends on a note of frustrated expectations. Mr. Kapasi and Mina Das both are doomed to return to their loveless marital lives—one, like a punctured balloon, back to the inescapable, invincible silence resultant of domestic discordance and the other without any remedy for her gnawing past. Jhumpa reveals the façade of conjugal relationship in this story of a bourgeois couple and a tour guide who is misguided by the signals, misinterpreted by himself.

"The Blessed House" is the story of the hasty marriage of 27 years old lackadaisical Twinkle and a 33 years old ambitious young man Sanjeev who is soon going to be corporate vice-president. What is common between them? They both like P.G.

Wodehouse and they both dislike Sitar music. In the second month of their marriage, Sanjeev notices that his wife has not grown out of her childhood. She cooks without recipes and feels no hurry to unpack the boxes in their new home. Her 'content yet curious' disposition drives her husband crazy. She hits upon a whole treasure of religious assortment left behind by the previous tenants. When Twinkle discovers a white porcelain Christ, St. Francis postcards and Noah's ark light-switch plates, she takes a fancy to them and wants to put a plaster virgin Mary on their front lawn. Sanjeev underestimates the tenacity of his wife's whims and in a showdown, threatens to dispose of the plaster idol. But when he notices that "some of the water, dripping down her hard blue face was tears" (149), he has to give in. Twinkle's fancy for this 'treasure-hunt' takes an absurd tun when their guests at the house-warming party indulge in this hunt. She finds a solid silver bust by Christ which Sanjeev knows, no matter what she promises; she will keep on the centre of the mantel, very much against his wish. He hates the bust but he loves her whims, nor do we know how long the beauty and charm of the wife will keep this marriage form falling apart; but Jhumpa, while underlining the temperamental incompatibility of the couple, seems to favour a humane attitude, full of compassion and kindness which has the power of cementing the marital bond.

The poignant sense of cultural transition and loss is not the only thing Mrs. Sen in the story "Mrs. Sen's" is suffering from; it is the lack of understanding and emotional support from her husband which makes the alien environment all the more painful and unpalatable to her. It is significant that Jhumpa Lahiri's women characters are fast-rooted in Indian culture or at least they have stronger links with India than her male characters. Shobha in "A Temporary Matter", Mrs. Sen in "Mrs. Sen's", and Mala in "The Third and Final Continent" miss their original country in varying degrees but male characters exhibit greater flexibility and adaptability. Mrs. Sen's haunting loneliness compels her to ask Eliot, the boy of whom she is the after-school caretaker whether he will put his mother in a nursing home when she is old. The boy replies that in that case, he would visit her every day. At this Mrs. Sen says:

> you say that now, but you will see, when you are a man, your life will be in places you cannot know now... you will miss one day, and another, and then she will have to drag herself on to a bus to get herself a bag of lozenges. (132)

Mrs. Sen's anguish is not caused only by the fact that she is reluctant arrival who had to come to America because of her husband's job as a teacher of mathematics at an American university, her pain would have been alleviated to a certain extent had her husband, who is by no means a hard-hearted person, shown more understanding and sympathy for her emotional struggle to cope with an alien world. This indifference and detachment allow a certain coldness between them which is suggested with subtlety:

> Eliot looked through the tiny window in the camera and waited for Mr. and Mrs. Sen to move closer together, but they didn't. They didn't hold hands or put their arms around each other's waists. Both smiled with their mouths closed, squinting into the wind. (130)

"Sexy" is also a story of fragile marital and extra-marital relations. An American girl Miranda sleepwalks into a relationship with a married Indian, Dev who compliments her as sexy. Miranda is brought to her senses by Rohin, the son of estranged Indian parents, who interprets the word sexy as loving somebody one does not know. She resolves to tell Dev "the things she had known all along, that it wasn't fair to her, or to his wife, that they both deserved better, that there was no point in dragging it on" (110). Marital fidelity which is so integral to Indian values is thrown to winds in the new world where the Indian yuppie male can get off at the airport with the woman who was sitting with him in the plane and call his wife to bid goodbye.

It is with neither objection nor enthusiasm, that the narrator in "The Third and Final Continent" marries Mala who could "cook, knit, embroider, sketch landscapes and recite poems by

Tagore" (181). She has been rejected, despite these talents, by a string of men as she does not possess a fair complexion. It is to save her from spinsterhood that her parents send their only child halfway across the world. Obviously, there is no warmth in the beginning of this relation. The narrator regards her arrival as that of "a coming month, or season—something inevitable, but meaningless at the time" (189). He waits to get used to her but a week later finds that they are still 'strangers'. He takes her to Mrs. Croft, his American landlady of over a hundred years old who scrutinizes Mala from top to toe and then declares her 'a perfect lady'—with this, the couple arrives. For the first time, they 'look' at each other and smile. Mala thus narrowly escapes the plight of Mrs. Sen. The narrator here feels what Mr. Sen ought to have felt:

> Like me, Mala had travelled far from home, not knowing where she was going, or what she would find, for no reason other than to be my wife. As strange as it seemed, I knew in my heart that one day her death would affect me, and stranger still, that mine would affect her. (195)

With this sympathy, the distance between the couple begins to lessen and the relation which begins with cool indifference is gradually warmed by love.

The images of marriage in the stories of Jhumpa Lahiri are diversified and multi-dimensional. She stresses the need to understand, to know, to communicate in order to strengthen the marital bond. She does not try to simplify the complexities within such a relationship. With elegance, subtlety and a rare insight, she records the emotional temperatures of her characters and comes out as a promising writer who with great sensitivity chronicles the successful or not so-successful attempts of building a home. It is not with the feministic approach that she does so, she seems to look upon marriage as an institution whose well-being determines the well-being of a larger social order. Especially against the backdrop of immigrant situation, these images of marriage assume an added significance, as they manifest the struggle to cope with the loss of tradition and the effort to cling to the reassurance of home.

NOTE

1. Jhumpa Lahiri, *Interpreter of Maladies* (New Delhi: HarperCollins, 1999), p. 12. All subsequent references have been incorporated into the text after quotations.

6

Immigrant Experience in Jhumpa Lahiri's *Interpreter of Maladies*

Exile plays a significant role in shaping Indian English sensibility. It is a complex evolutionary process entailing cross-cultural shifts, loss of mother tongue, native ethos combating with the militating elements of new environment and the dual pull of cultural loyalties. Indian English writing, due to its cross-culture origin, has intrinsically been revolving time and again around the theme of the compelling and challenging encounter between two cultures—apparently antagonistic in their attitudes, approaches and values. The immigrant experience is complicated as a sensitive immigrant finds himself or herself perpetually at a transit station fraught with the memories of the original home which are struggling with the realities of the new world. It is more so in the case of Indian women writers in English because most of them share the same cultural dichotomy. To name only a few, Kamala Markandeya is married to an English man and settled in England; there is Ruth Prawar Zhabvalla of Polish parentage who has her upbringing in Germany and education in England and is married to an Indian architect; there is Anita Desai who has a German mother and a Bengali father and there is Bharati Mukherjee who rejects a hyphenated identity and has avowedly become one of the Americans. Jhumpa Lahiri, who has attracted attention by her Pulitzer winning debut collection of stories—*Interpreter of Maladies* is the latest writer in this league. Born in London in 1967 and raised in Rhodes Islands, she lives in New York. West is her home, though her parents are born and raised in India. Her stories record the experiences of both first- and second-generation Indian immigrants and majority of her characters, like her, have relatives in India but their home, in unambiguous terms, is northeastern United States. However, her stories evince that the racial and cultural memory is very much at work and 'feeling at home' remains a difficult task.

The sense of cultural tradition and loss finds a poignant expression in "Mrs. Sen's" where the title character is seen through the eyes of an American eleven year-old, son of a single parent. A thirty year-old wife of a mathematics professor, Mrs. Sen is a reluctant arrival who becomes the after-school caretaker for a young boy, Eliot. Eliot observes the daily rituals that connect her to her past as she misses her family and finds the northeastern United States to be overwhelming and unfriendly. The mention of the word 'India' seems to release something in her. "She, too, looked around the room, as if she noticed in the lampshades, in the teapot, in the shadows frozen on the carpet, something the rest of them could not.... Everything is there."[1] Eliot develops a liking for her; not only because Mrs. Sen's apartment is warm but also there is warmth of affection. Through her memories, he too gets a glimpse of India as he comes to understand that "when Mrs. Sen said home, she meant India" (116). Home is a memory, a longing, a need for her where she wants to turn for those things with which she is familiar—language, food, social relations and traditions, rituals, ceremonies and cultural values. In a reminiscent mood, she tells Eliot of weddings in her family when women laugh and gossip and slice fifty kilos of vegetables through the night and their chatter makes it impossible to fall asleep those nights, and she says: "Here, in this place where Mr. Sen has brought me. I cannot sometimes sleep in so much silence" (115). One day while cutting vegetables she asks Eliot if he thinks the neighbours would come to her help if she were to scream at the top of her lungs. "May be", he says and adds that more likely they would just call to complain about the noise. She then explains to him that, "At home that is all you have to do. Not everybody has a telephone. But just raise your voice a bit, or express grief or joy of any kind, and one whole neighbourhood and half of another has come to share the news, to help with arrangements" (116).

This makes Eliot think about his home and the fact that he has never talked to his neighbours. It is evident that Mrs. Sen's loneliness emanates from being so far from home whereas the boy's loneliness comes from living in suburbia. It is caused by the fact that he does not know his father and hardly knows his mother. When Mrs. Sen asks whether he misses his mother in the afternoons, he finds that the thought has never even occurred to him. She comes to this sad realisation that he is wiser as he is already acclimatized to the pain that afflicts her.

The story titled "The Third and Final Continent" presents the other side of the complex immigrant experience. It unfolds itself on two levels: how the protagonist, a 36 year-old Bengali, and his 103 year-old American landlady who is fierce, independent and idiosyncratic, learn and grow from the experience of each other and secondly, how the narrator gradually overcomes the growing sense of alienation and loneliness and learns the ways of the new world. Both these stories present different gender reactions to the diasporic experience. Mrs. Sen's stubborn refusal to learn driving can be seen as a subconscious way of her resistance to the dictated terms of this new world. Contrary to this, the narrator in "The Third and Final Continent", patiently and painstakingly, develops a taste not only for American cornflakes but for American life as well and while doing so he remains firmly grounded in his culture. The process of survival has not been easy even for him as he looks back to it with a sense of bewilderment:

> I am not the only man to seek his fortune far from home, and certainly I am not the first. Still, there are times I am bewildered by each mile I have traveled, each meal I have eaten, each person I have known, each room in which I have slept. As ordinary as it all appears, there are times when it is beyond my imagination. (198)

And then there is also a sense of uneasiness about the next generation which is born and brought up in America and is culturally displaced. The narrator says:

> We have a son who attends Harvard University. Mala no longer drapes the end of her sari over her head, or weeps

> at night for her parents, but occasionally she weeps for our son. So we drive to Cambridge to visit him, or bring him home for a week end, so that he can eat rice with us with his hands, and speak in Bengali, things we sometimes worry he will no longer do after we die. (197)

If Mrs. Sen is seen through the eyes; of an eleven years old boy. Mr. Pirzada, in the story "When Mr. Pirzada came to Dine" is observed by a ten year-old girl. The immigrant experience when filtered through the juvenile consciousness in the stories of Jhumpa Lahiri, acquires a remarkable sensitivity. Mr. Pirzada belongs to Dacca which is going through a crucial phase due to Bangladesh war and from where he has not heard a word of his wife and seven daughters. He comes to visit Lilia's parents regularly, who are Indian immigrants. The compatriots huddle together in an alien country and our narrator—this little girl notices that before eating Mr. Pirzada takes out a plain silver watch from his pocket and keeps it on the coffee table. This pocket watch is set to the local time in Dacca which is eleven hours ahead. She says:

> When I saw it that night, as he wound it and arranged it on the coffee table, an uneasiness possessed me: life, I realised, was being lived in Dacca first. I imagined Mr. Pirzada's daughters rising from sleep, tying ribbons in their hair, anticipating breakfast, preparing for school. Our meals, our actions were only a shadow of what had already happened there, a lagging ghost of where Mr. Pirzada really belonged. (30-31)

The anguish of the out-of-context lives of immigrants like Mr. Pirzada and Mrs. Sen is similar as Mrs. Sen also keeps listening to the recorded voices of her relatives on a tape, informing Eliot that "these are things that happened the day I left India" (128), thus she resorts to memory for self-preservation, seeking shelter in the past which seems incredibly attractive because it does not change and therefore offers a refuge from the turbulence of the flux—that is present. It seems that perhaps the span of a short story does not give Lahiri much space to explore some more involved and complicated nuances of the immigrant situation. For example, Mrs. Sen's anguish and her poignant sense of loss of the familiar is expressed with uncommon sensitivity but if she, who believes that "Everything is in India" were to go back in search of her original home, she would have been in for a terrible shock. Probably, she would find that her neighbourhood has forgotten her and it is no longer interested in reviving the acquaintance. Original home, the memory of which becomes a psychic repository for the essence of one's cultural self, may turn out to be an illusion after all, because society is rushing head over heels toward the future, and the home, due to a number of multiple forces, may be a space—fractured and splintered beyond recognition. This is the tragedy of greater dimensions and perhaps Jhumpa Lahiri would delve deep into it in some novel.

The pang of loss is somewhat alleviated in case of second-generation Indian immigrants. In stories like "This Blessed House", "Sexy" and "A Temporary Matter" characters are grappling with marriages that have gone wrong. Themes of emotional struggles of love, relationships, communication against the backdrop of immigrant experience, are handled with deftness in these stories. These second-generation immigrants belong to the upper middle-class. They work in offices and spend their excess money in high-end stores. Their children suffer from their having become westernized. None of these characters is struggling to survive in an alien land therefore their problems are of a different nature. One hopes to read more about their world in some future novel by Jhumpa Lahiri. Even the title story "Interpreter of Maladies" is more about the need for understanding, communication and faltering marriage than about the encounter between an Indian and Indian-Americans. Some of these second-generation Indian-Americans are yuppie like characters, like Dev in "Sexy", who meets an American girl Miranda while shopping for his Indian wife in a store and starts an affair with her. The futility of this relationship dawns on her only through the child of an estranged Indian couple whose father has abandoned his mother because on a flight from Delhi to Montreal, he fell in love with another woman, an

English girl, half his age and instead of flying home to his wife and son, he got off with the woman at the Heathrow.

Jhumpa Lahiri's fictional interpretation of the immigrant situation is marked by her attempt to observe and understand the characters caught in the parallax of this double perspective—between the ancient traditions of her ancestors and the sometimes baffling prospects of the new world. Living on an ethnic divide, her characters try to change and find that the more they try, the more they remain the same. They struggle to survive in the baffling new world while suffering from the threat under which the old relationships and old ways of life are coming. Her stories represent a different type of expatriate writing as she is a descendant of indentured immigrants and the culture clash operates on various levels. It is also significant that displacement and loss of one's cultural self still exerts a powerful pull on the imagination of Indian-Americans who are themselves distant from the actual experience of displacement. Memories of the trials and tribulations of survival, experienced by the first-generation immigrants, is still a mine of material for them. And it is a perennial source because the last two decades have seen high levels of emigration from Asian countries. Their experience of a simultaneous existence in two cultures is a subtle one and invites them to express it in a variety of ways. One hopes that the promise and potential she has shown in this debut collection of stories will culminate into more penetrating and sensitive chronicles of the diasporic experience with all its dimensions and complexities.

NOTE

1. Jhumpa Lahiri. *Interpreter of Maladies* (New Delhi: HarperCollins Publishers India Pvt. Ltd., 1999), p. 113. Subsequent references to this book have been incorporated in the text itself after quotes.

7

Images of Women in Exile

> Migration and dispersion are natural phenomena, widely familiar both in the world of plants and in the animal kingdom. Human beings have been no exception.[1]

Immigrants are the people who migrate to foreign countries and experience a sense of loss there. They feel themselves lost in that alien land and alien culture. With a number of Indians migrating to foreign countries, we need to understand the psyche of the immigrants, the conditions and problems they face, and the struggle they face for their identity. Thus, this discussion on the diasporics becomes all the more relevant.

Diasporic writers live on the margin of the two societies and cultures, transforming their experience about the 'mother' and the 'other' country in their writings. Jasbir Jain thinks diaspora is not just a matter of dislocation or deterritorialisation, but an experience made-up of collectivities, multiple journeys, still points and border crossings. Various women diasporic writers have portrayed this experience through their women expatriate characters in their novels.

In the Indian context, woman is quintessentially immigrant. She is continuously displaced, and the process of uprootment and re-rootment is her predicament. In this sense, the Sanskrit term '*Dwij*' (twice born) is apt for her. Therefore, the immigrant experience of women characters is all the more poignant. Present chapter discusses the clash that women in migration suffer from. Their reaction to the bicultural pull; their sense of dislocation and belonging to nowhere; and their transformation and evolvement are the major issues this paper is concerned with.

Bharati Mukherjee, Jhumpa Lahiri and Manju Kapur have explored and portrayed the struggle, evolvement and survival of the women in exile. When a woman writes about a woman, she depicts all those dimensions of migration that she herself has experienced. And thus the description becomes all the more authentic and axiomatic.

Lahiri's book *The Namesake* is mainly concerned with the second-generation diasporics but it also highlights the plight of a woman—Ashima Ganguli—who migrates to US after getting married to Ashoke Ganguli. Manju Kapur in her novel *The Immigrant* quotes very aptly for her protagonist Nina:

> the immigrant who comes as a wife has a more difficult time. If work exists for her, it is in the future, and after much finding of feet. At present all she is, is a wife, and a wife is alone for many, many hours. There will come a day when even books are powerless to distract. When the house and its convenience can no longer completely charm or compensate. Then she realises she is an immigrant for life. (Kapur, 124)

Ashima's case is no different. Her companions of the solitude are the letters from India, the Bengali novels and the *Desh* magazines brought along from India, and her household tasks like cooking and cleaning. But soon she realizes that her status of an immigrant is like her shadow that cannot be left behind.

The opening page of the book tells about Ashima trying to prepare a 'humble approximation' of an Indian snack using American ingredients. "Tasting from a cupped palm, she frowns; as usual, there's something missing" (1). This 'humble approximation' and 'something missing' are some of the main themes of the novel. "This is a frequently reduplicated gesture, and not only the 'snack', but all the Bengali rituals and ceremonies observed by the Gangulis in the States seem to become 'humble approximations' of the originals."[2]

There are many clashes that Ashima faces. She is reluctant to introduce second-hand appliances into her home in Boston. She, like a typical Indian wife, never says her husband's name. "Like a kiss or caress in a hindi movie, a husband's name is something intimate and therefore unspoken, cleverly patched over" (2). Ashima resembles with Jyoti of *Jasmine* who hesitates in uttering Prakash's name. She is a simple peasant girl who gets married to a city-bred boy Prakash and feels it difficult to cope with his modern thinking.

Ashima feels embarrassed to wear a knee-length gown in the hospital, feels awkward when a man says 'I love you' to his wife. Because these are the "Words Ashima has neither heard nor expects to hear from her husband; this is not the way they are" (3). Ashima, like other Indian children, had been a sheltered child. But things are different in America. In contrast to Judy and Alan who go out leaving Amber and Clover unsupervised; "it is the first time in her life she has slept alone, surrounded by strangers; all her life she has slept either in a room with her parents, or with Ashoke at her side" (3).

When Ashoke comes to see her for marriage, Ashima secretly slips into his shoes. This was her first stance of intimacy with her would-be husband. "Lingering sweat from the owner's feet mingled with hers, causing her heart to race; it was the closest thing she had ever experienced to the touch of a man" (8). Such a lady when comes to America, its hard for her to cope up with the new culture, the new surroundings. "She would be the most diasporic character-torn between histories, geographies and identities.... Neither in marriage, nor in the consequent displacement was there any space for her to assert herself."[3] At every moment she is reminded of India. "Caught between India and America, Ashima becomes 'homeless'—she can be 'at home' no where. The space she will inhabit, mentally, will be always somewhere in a 'liminal', in-between terrain—to belong where is tantamount to not to belong."[4] Just like Ashima, Tara too is a sheltered child, who gets everything just for asking. It is hard for her too to survive the struggle and differences in US.

When in America, Ashima is expecting her first baby she is too scared of it. She thinks "it's strange that her child will be born in a place most people enter either to suffer or to die" (4). In spite of her problems in surviving in America, what bothers her the most is—motherhood in a foreign land.

> For it was one thing to be pregnant,.... That it was happening so far from home, unmonitored and unobserved by those she loved, had made it more miraculous still. But she is terrified to raise a child in a country where she is related to no one, where she knows so little, where life seems so tentative and spare. (6)

Being outside one's homeland is as much painful as giving birth. Lahiri herself considers migration as rebirth. When a person migrates, he gives birth to a new self. But when a woman migrates its a lifelong process of adaptation:

> ...being a foreigner...is a sort of lifelong pregnancy—a perpetual wait, a constant burden, a continuous feeling out of sorts. It is an ongoing responsibility, a parenthesis in what had once been ordinary life, only to discover that the previous life has vanished, replaced by something more complicated and demanding...is something that elicits the same curiosity from strangers, the same combination of pity and respect. (49-50)

In *Jasmine*, we find a path-finder, who finds her way through dense problems and moves on as if living a new life. In Jasmine's odyssey, we have some glimpses of Bharati Mukherjee herself. Mukherjee says in an interview: "I have been murdered and reborn at least three times, the very correct young woman I was trained to be, and was very happy being, is very different from the politicized, shrill, civil rights activist I was in Canada, and from the urgent writer that I have become in the last few years in the United States."[5]

To survive, Jasmine too, murders and rebirths herself for a number of times. What she confides in the novel seems to be a replica of Mukherjee's statement: "There are no harmless, compassionate ways to remake oneself. We murder who we were so we can rebirth ourselves—in the images of dreams" (29).

Jasmine begins with an astrologer prophesying the "widowhood and exile" of the child Jyoti, which she denies. Although it happens, yet even then how Jyoti struggles, fights, adapts and survives, is the main concern of this novel. She undergoes many transformations from Jyoti to Jasmine, to Jase, to Jane, and during her every role she rebels, revolts and transforms. All through the novel she gets uprooted and re-rooted for a number of times, and finally ends with leaving her live-in, disabled partner Bud, in order to join Taylor, her companion of Manhattan.

She says "I changed myself because I wanted to. To bunker oneself inside nostalgia...was to be a coward" (185). Its her courage that she is not only able to strike the roots easily, but also to uproot herself with equal ease and move on without any remorse. "A boundary is not that at which something stops but, as the Greek recognized, the boundary is that from which something begins its presencing."[6] The quote is befitting for Jasmine. She begins her presencing, her new identities at the boundary rather than stopping there.

Tara and Jasmine have nothing in common except their creator. Tara emigrated to Vassar at an early age of fifteen to study further because her father—the Bengal Tiger—thought of Calcutta as no longer a safe place. But for Tara, who 'had never been farther than Shambazar', 'Vassar had been an almost unsalvageable mistake'. On the other hand, Jasmine migrated to US in order to be a 'Sati' (burn herself) in the campus of the university her husband wanted to study in. She moves on with no money and with forged papers. For Tara 'in Calcutta the chauffer had always carried smelling salts for her in the glove compartment', while for Jyoti her grandmother says to her father, 'you're going to have to wear out your sandals getting rid of this one'. Such was the difference between them. When Tara leaves India, she moves on with pleasant memories in her rucksack and feels nostalgic in Vassar. While Jasmine moves not to come back or feel nostalgic about India. In *The Tiger's Daughter*,

> Mukherjee sets about exposing how it feels for a fifteen-year-old girl to leave a sheltered home hedged by class

> privilege and wealth, come back to it grown to a young womanhood—to come home after breaking all the social taboos by marrying a foreigner—and see whether she can find her place at home again.[7]

Tara is unable to find her place in India as well as in America. She feels homesick in America and prays to Goddess Kali for strength. She desires to become a part of her new surroundings, but she is unable to uproot herself. In turn, she becomes a hybrid identity; becomes a victim of clash of ideologies of India and America. In the terms of Mukherjee's husband Clark Blaise, she was incapable of the *unhousement* and *rehousement*:

> She lacks the capacity to probe into the differences between the two cultures, accept the merits of both or one, and then adopt the necessary changes. Hence she fails to feel at home in spite of her best intentions.[8]

In an attempt to Americanize herself, she hastily marries David Cartwright, who is wholly Western and cannot feel oneness with Tara. He misunderstands her affection and longing for her family as her overdependence, and thus despises it. Tara is unable to strike her roots, and David is unable to understand it. In spite of her being a modern lady, somewhere within, she too is a deep-rooted Indian who gets depressed on seeing her friends in swimsuits during the picnic at Bengal Tiger's factory. She thinks that "the soft edges of their bottoms escaping the grip of the western bathing suit had no business being seen by the servants" (115). Living in America she yearns for India and tries to create an India of her own:

> On days she had thought she could not possibly survive, she had shaken out all silk scarves, ironed them and hung them to make the apartment more "Indian". She had curried hamburger desperately till David's stomach had protested...she had burnt incense sent from home, till the hippie neighbors began to take an undue interest in her. (41-42)

But she fails to feel at home in spite of all her efforts. She tries to acculturate herself in the new culture, even marries a foreigner, but before she could acculturate she has the urge of contra-acculturation.

> Tara...finds it difficult to relate herself to her family, city, culture in general since her marriage to an American, her Western education are enough *signs* to brand her as an 'alienated' westernized woman. The implicit logic is that since she is exposed to the west and has absorbed its values she must be necessarily alienated. Therefore, even when she tries to 'voice' her continuing attachment for and identity with India, the voice doesn't carry conviction.[9]

Homi K. Bhabha, in "Of Mimicry and Man: The Ambivalence of Colonial Discourse" discusses the concept of Mimicry. He talks that the colonial encounter between the white presence and its black semblance gives rise to the question of the ambivalence of mimicry. An ideological ambivalence is present everywhere, every time, with every immigrant. They are hybrid identities according to Bhabha's concept, who possess traits of both the cultures but actually are neither Indian nor American Ashima is the only character out of these four, who is least touched by the Western traits. Tara remains confused while Nina and Jasmine find a new place. Manju Kapur asserts: "For an immigrant there was no going back.... When one was reinventing oneself, anywhere could be home. Pull up your shallow roots and move. Find a new place, new friends, a new family. It had been possible once, it would be possible again" (333-34). Tara is a true hybrid; Ashima is transnational and transcultural in character; Jasmine and Nina show the traits of existentialism and acculturation. We find disparate images of women in the works of these women writers.

Manju Kapur has pointed out another major problem that a lady faces while migrating. Nina struggles at the airport to prove that she is legally married. She sighs, "...you are deceived, and you have deceived me. You made it out to be a liberal haven where everybody loved you. This woman is looking for a reason to get rid of me. I am the wrong colour, I come from the wrong place. See me in this airport, of all the passengers the only one not allowed to sail through immigration, made to feel like an illegal alien. See, see, see" (108). She feels as if she is a criminal and "does not like her introduction to the new world" (109). Still she manages to get out of this.

In India, almost all the girls are trained and raised to be adaptable as daughters, wives and mothers. This sense of adaptability helps them when they migrate to a foreign land. Mukherjee also states the same in one of her interviews: "The kind of women I write about...are those who are adaptable. We've all been raised to please, been trained to be adaptable as wives, and that adaptability is working to the women's advantage when we come over as immigrants."[10]

In Indian context, women are always supposed to obey the men. The earliest metrical work of Hinduism—*Manusmriti* states: "A girl, a young woman, or even an old woman should not do anything independently, even in her own house. In childhood a woman should be under her father's control, in youth under her husband's and when her husband is dead, under her sons."[11] Some unknown author has very rightly said, "Women have been taught that, for us, the earth is flat, and that if we venture out, we will fall off the edge." Under this impression Ashima, Jasmine and Nina start their journey with this advantage of adaptation, but all of them end it at different destinations.

Lahiri says in "My Two Lives", "In spite of the first lessons of arithmetic, one plus one did not equal two but zero, my conflicting selves always canceling each other out."[12] The two selves—before and after migration—of these characters also overpower each other and in turn lose both the identities.

All the four characters suffer from the same clash but their reactions towards it are different. Ashima not only survives but also keeps her Indianness intact in her. Tara becomes a poor victim of this clash. In order to uproot herself she even marries an American but doesn't succeed. Comes back to India in search of her nostalgic dream but unable to cope with the changed India, gets defiled by Tuntunwala and decides to go back. Jasmine migrates to fulfill a weird dream of hers, but once in America forgets about it and transforms drastically.

After her rape she doesn't halt and lament, rather she kills the demon and moves ahead. Lives various lives, asserts her identity and becomes an altogether new personality, who in spite of her Indianness has the courage to leave her partner and father of the child she is carrying, in order to accompany her lover. Nina, on the other hand, tries hard to acculturate into the new culture with all its odds and the odds of her husband's sexual limitations. But soon gets engaged with a foreigner, and finally leaves Ananda to find her own identity in the new land which is no more alien to her. Different women, different stories, yet all of them are governed by their womanly instinct. Due to better adaptability, they do strike the roots, but the impact of this acculturation remains with them for long, and they realize that no matter how acculturated they are, the bicultural pull that they face; their sense of universality or the sense of belonging to more than one place and also the sense of dislocation or the feeling of belonging to nowhere is quite overwhelming. They suffer, struggle, and survive in their own ingenious ways and go through the complex processes of rejection and acceptance, overcoming ambivalence, and finally come to terms with the new reality of an alien ambience. Their endurance, grit and enterprise endear them to us and win our admiration not only for themselves, but also for their creators.

NOTES

1. N. Jayaram, "Introduction: The Study of Indian Diaspora" in *The Indian Diaspora: Dynamics of Migration.* New Delhi: Sage Publications, 2004, p. 15.
2. Nigamananda Das, *Jhumpa Lahiri—Critical Perspectives.* New Delhi: Pencraft International, 2008, p. 30.
3. *Ibid.*, pp. 29-30.
4. *Ibid.*, p. 32.
5. Michael Connel, Grearson Jessi and Grimes Tom, "An Interview with Bharati Mukherjee," *Iowa Review* 20, 3(1990), p. 18.
6. Martin Heidgger, "Building, Dwelling, Thinking" in *Poetry, Language, Thought.* New York: Harper & Row, 1975, p. 154.

* Co-writer of this essay is Mrs. Vibha Singh Tomar, Asstt. Prof., Humanities, SVITS, Ujjain.

7. Nagendra Kumar, *Cultural Conflict in the Fiction of Bharati Mukherjee*. New Delhi: Atlantic Publishers, 2001, pp. 41-42.
8. Indira Nityanandam, *Three Great Indian Women Novelists*. New Delhi: Creative Books, 2000, p. 65.
9. M. Sivaramkrishna, "Bharati Mukherjee" in M.S. Prasad, ed. *Indian English Novelists*. New Delhi: Sterling, 1982, p. 74.
10. Michael Connel et al. "An Interview with Bharati Mukherjee," p. 25.
11. *Manusmriti* (http://www.suite101.com/article.cfm/woman_in_india/81390).
12. Jhumpa Lahiri, "My Two Lives" (http://www.desilit.org/weblog/archives/2006/02).

8

Escape of the Dead: A Study of Manju Kapur's *Difficult Daughters*

> The Shade of the dead escapes from the funeral pyre and returns to our midst.
>
> —Propertius

Surely, they do escape and return—in the abode of literature which hardly makes any discrimination between the dead and the living. Virmati returns as the narrator in *Difficult Daughters* starts piecing together material from muddled memories, imagining and molding history and thereby reconstructing the 'connection' between herself and her dead mother. The novel is an attempt to discover the woman who happened to the narrator's mother. It is a sort of masonry of the narrator who, with her head and heart construct a mansion where the dead could live. It is in the backdrop of the complex mother-daughter relationship that this endeavour to reconstitute the life of Virmati should be seen. The tone is set right in the beginning: "The one thing I had wanted was not to be like my mother" (1). But what was her mother like? The novel attempts to answer this question. It has been an uneasy relationship, further complicated by the alternating currents of love and hate. Looking at the photograph of her departed mother, the narrator is unable to "remember a time it had been right between us and the guilt that her life kept in check now overwhelmed me" (2). She is haunted by her mother's question: "Why do you deliberately misunderstand me?" The need to understand, to fathom the intricate workings of the heart, to come to terms with the woman hidden behind a "silent, brisk, and bad-tempered" (2) mother propels the narrator to her odyssey that takes her from pillar to post in search of Virmati.

Still, *Difficult Daughters* is not a mere fictional biography and objectivity does not seem to be a cherished ideal, as the picture that emerges is coloured by the experience and imagination of the narrator. The scattered facts about Virmati's life and times are selected and processed by her and therefore in revealing Virmati she also reveals herself apparently remaining modestly in the background.

The craving to be understood properly and the anguish of being misunderstood lies at the nucleus of this novel. Kasturi does not understand her daughter Virmati's need for affection, the eldest of her eleven children who is burdened with the unsolicited motherhood of her siblings:

> At times Virmati yearned for affection, for some sign that she was special. However, when she put her head next to the youngest baby, feeding in the mother's arms, Kasturi would get irritated and push her away. (6)

This lack of understanding leads Virmati to an illicit affair with a married man who gives her the feeling of being 'special'. The question is: has she learnt any lesson from her own life? In her *avatar* of the mother of a growing-up daughter, she shows the same lack of understanding when she tightens her reins on Ida—the narrator—"She said it was for my own good. As a result, I am constantly looking for escape routes" (258).

Virmati may be a difficult daughter so far as her refusal to marry the man her family has chosen is concerned but beyond that she is neither a rebel nor an iconoclast or a seeker of new paths who runs the risk of defying an outdated social structure demanding conformity at the cost of one's identity or independence. Independence, within or without marriage is hardly a coveted state for her. Her so-called passion for further studies is merely a ruse for her to stall marriage, thereby buying more time to linger in the impossible situation she had landed herself into, by walking into the trap of Harish—a professor of English literature. Married to an illiterate wife whose existence centres round her culinary skills and keeping the house clean, the professor ceaselessly professes his love for her, writes loveletters to her and ultimately Virmati gives into his overtures. Even this refusal of her fiancé and falling in love with the professor is not a case of her choice or an assertion of her will. Torn between duty and desire, Virmati lacks the nerve to inform her family about her affair with the professor. When she is finally unable to postpone her marriage with her fiancé any longer, her desperate search for escapes takes her to the suicidal attempt which is aborted just in time—much to the embarrassment of her Aryasamaji family which advocated female education even in the pre-independence era. She is locked in the godown from where she continues correspondence with her lover. Through this correspondence we are made aware of the fact that the professor's wife has become pregnant and this leaves Virmati heart broken. She eventually decides to pursue her studies and goes to Lahore. The professor tries to explain the situation by saying that he does not live with his wife in any 'meaningful' way and the "co-wives are part of our social traditions" (112). But as the professor's friend claims she will "come round eventually" (110); a dismayed reader finds that she actually does. Insincere to both these women and conventionally two-timing—this man is not only hoodwinking his illiterate wife but also Virmati who is educated and is troubled by the misgivings about her lover's integrity. But those doubts notwithstanding, the professor successfully makes her surrender to his sexual advances. Virmati's only demand is: "Marry me and make it clear to everybody" (114). We are reminded of Virmati's grouse that her family gives more importance to her marriage than her independence (106). Is it her idea of being independent? Isn't she running away from an arranged marriage just to covet another—and this time with a married man—depriving his wife and children of their rights and place? She does not show any nerve to resist the professor's overtures in the same manner as she had resisted her parents when they wanted to marry her off. Obviously, Virmati might be a difficult daughter but as a woman—she has been very timid and unassertive. At this plane, we are unable to find any significant difference between an educated and enlightened Virmati and professor's illiterate housewife Ganga.

And the ironical backdrop for this personal drama in Virmati's life in India's struggle for independence and the tragic partition. Virmati, like her friend Swarnalata and her cousin

Shakuntala—does not have any 'fruitful engagement with the world'. She is acutely aware of her position and suffers some transitory phases of guilt and depression. Her self-assessment rings quite true as she blurts out in the heated exchange with the professor:

> I break my engagement because of you, blacken my family's name, am locked up inside my house, get sent to Lahore because no one knows what to do with me. Here I am in the position of being your secret wife, full of shame, wondering what people will say if they find out, not being able to live in peace, study in peace...and Why? Because I am an idiot. (137)

That Virmati's notions of independence are merely the ways of self-delusion is obvious from the fact that a life without marriage is 'strange' and 'not quite right' to her and she is not sure that she is capable of leading a 'lonely life'.

On this score, is there any radical difference between the thinking of her family and her own? Swarnalata, her activist friend exhorts her, "Marriage is not the only thing in life, Viru. The War—the Satyagraha movement—because of these things, women are coming out of their homes. Taking jobs, fighting, and going to jail. Wake up from your stable dream" (139).

Clearly, this idea is unpalatable to her. When Swarnalata suggests her to participate in Satyagraha—she immediately is reminded of her family and becomes concerned about their reaction. How convenient it is to forget the same family in matrimonial affairs and suddenly become worried about its possible reaction when it comes to fight for a noble cause. About this time, she finds herself pregnant and in order to get here pregnancy terminated she deceives her family by asking for a pair of gold bangles as she has to arrange money. The conclusion she draws from the traumatic experience is confounding once against: She was his for life, whether he ever married her or not. Her body was marked by him. She could never look elsewhere, never entertain another choice—something she does not know anything about. Not only the professor lands her into this extremely difficult situation, his unexpected and indiscrete visit to Nahan—where she has a decent job—forces her to leave the decent job she has there. On her way to Shanti Niketan, she drops in the house of poet friend of the professor and the poet friend's insistence does not leave any room for the professor to evade and he has to marry Virmati. It is noteworthy that it is not Virmati's persuasion, but the way the poet friend hustles this affair that the marriage takes place. But for the situation, Virmati would have lived the life of a mistress.

But marriage hardly solves Virmati's problems. There she has to face the resistance of Ganga, the professor's first wife who rules over the kitchen and other household affairs whereas Virmati has to be content only by sharing bed with the professor. When the riots of partition start in Amritsar; taking advantage of Ganga and her children's departure, Virmati gives away their clothes to the needy people in the Camps. She summons a locksmith who breaks open Ganga's cupboard. "Just seeing those sarees made her sic. Each one of them reminded her of the woman, with her round face, round bindi and a black kajal-lined eyes starting fixedly at her with loathing" (225). And he sweeps away everything that belongs to Ganga and gives away in charity; as if she is trying to wipe away her existence. Ganga's return never takes place and we find that when it comes to stake her rights, Virmati's sense of justice deserts here and she usurps Ganga's place, unscrupulously and without compunction.

So this is the picture of Virmati that emerges from the narrative—timid, value, confused, insecure, unsure, unassertive, but sometimes stubborn, jealous and even sly—not at all an inspiring figures, yet every inch a human being. Driven by the emotions beyond her control, her suffering stems from her being difficult not only to her parents but also to herself. Hat is significant is that in the portrayal of Virmati, Ida—her daughter and the narrator of her story is not explicitly judgmental; there is an unmistakably honesty which illumines the rounded character of Virmati with its multi-dimensional complexities. She expresses her wish to donate her body after he death—may be that way she tries to seek perpetuity after death but more than it is her craving to be 'valued', "When I die, she said to me, I want my body donated. My eyes, my heart, my kidneys, any organ that can be of use. That way someone will value me after I have gone" (1).

But, contrary to her wishes, she is burnt with her organs intact. Why this does happen, we do not know and the narrator does not tell us but Virmati lives and dies without proper recognition and evaluation—this much becomes obvious. The novel seems to be an effort by way of compensation on the part of the narrator. One wishes that the narrator had given some more intensity and detail to the mother-daughter relationship which is suggested through very few strokes. They provide a vantage point to view Virmati as the events unfold the woman lurking behind a mother. "Without her, I am lost, I look for ways to connect," (3) says the narrator. And the novel connects them by the way it points to the ways of their becoming 'difficult' daughters.

Virmati wants Ida to be a model daughter who questions that why it is so important to please her father? Under pressure to perform day and night she also seeks escape and plunges into a disastrous marriage—incurring further disapproval of her mother. To snap out of her complexes and to discover her mother who haunted her throughout—Ida, the daughter and the narrator; builds like a wordsmith a mansion—this novel; to shelter the dead:

> All through, I felt the excitement of discovery, the pleasure of fitting narratives into a discernible inheritance. This books weaves a connection between my mother and me, each word a brick in a mansion I made with my head and my heart. Now live in it, Mama, and leave me be. Do not haunt me anyone. (259)

But will that actually happen? The doubt lingers as the dead are slippery; they do escape and continue to haunt. The 'liberation' of the writer (if it is not an illusion) transforms into the 'possession' of the reader. Difficult daughters continue to inhabit our experience and imagination.

REFERENCE

Kapur, Manju. *Difficult Daughters*. New Delhi: Penguin Books, 1998. Parenthetical page numbers refer to this edition.

9

Arun Kolatkar's *Jejuri*

Commonwealth Poetry Prize winner poem *Jejuri* (1976) by Arun Kolatkar has been a poem that can be termed as the Indian 'Wasteland'. Jejuri, thirty miles from Pune has one of the most prominent temples in western Maharashtra and it is dedicated to the God known as 'Mallari Martand'. Khandoba is worshipped by people of all castes and creeds. Divided into many small poems this poem is a composite whole.

The first question that arises is: why the narrator goes to Jejuri? Is a religious quest the chief motive behind the narrator's journey to Jejuri? Generally, *Jejuri* is regarded as a quest poem. It is, undoubtedly, a presentation of modern urban skepticism impinging upon ancient religious tradition. According to M.K. Naik, the thematic complex is much larger and the poem is a "conscious attempt to present in sharp contrast three major value-systems—viz. those of ancient religious tradition, modern Industrial civilization and—a value system older than both these—the Life Principle in Nature and its ways."[1]

The poem is full of the pictures of aridity and ugliness, decay and neglect, fossilization and perversion. The ironic description in these lines makes it clear:

> "The little town/ With its sixty three priests inside their sixty three houses/ huddled at the foot of the hill/ with its three hundred pillars five hundred steps and eighteen arches." These 'wretched' hills have nothing to show except 'sand blasted shoulders bladed with shale', 'Lime stone Lions', 'cactus fang', 'thighs of sand stone' and

'pelvic granite'. The poem 'Water Supply' offers a picture of a dry water tap which looks like 'a brass mouse with a broken neck' and 'The Reservoir' clearly states that "There is not a drop of water/ in the great reservoir the Peshvas built/ There is nothing in it/ Except a hundred years of silt." Various stages of dilapidation are seen in the temples on the hills. "The roof comes down on Maruti's head" and "a mongrel bitch has found a place/ for herself and her puppies/ in the heart of the ruin." In a temple the heavy door hangs on one hinge alone 'Like the local drunk'; The Temple Rat, "Stops on the mighty shoulder/ of the warrior god/ for a quick look around."

In Kolatkar's poems inanimate objects often form a parallel world and constantly try to defeat the human beings. Their behaviour often assumes the ironical human ways. Therefore, the bus when it comes "stands/ purring softly in front of the priest/ A catgrin on its face/ and a live ready to eat pilgrim/ held between its teeth!" The priest, his young son, the traditional temple attendants and the hangers on—they are all drawn in accordance with the general mood of the poem. The priest's son, a school boy, acts as a guide, since his school has vacation, and when asked whether he believes in the legend of the place: "he does not reply/ but merely looks uncomfortable/ shrugs and looks away."

Jejuri has evoked mixed reactions. It has been called "a poem of extraordinary qualities."[2] "A poem that depicts symbolically the tortured psyche of modern man."[3] "An X-ray vision of the enveloping dilapidation and the poet's reaction to it."[4] But there are critics who question Kolatkar's treatment of the theme and also his intentions in writing this poem. For example, we have Marathi critics like Ravindra Kimbahune and Bhalchandra Nemade who think that the poem is primarily written for the amusement of foreign readers. "It tempers with the native reality and tries to distort it in such a manner as to please the foreign readers."[5] In their opinion, the attention of the poet is fixed to the symbols of dilapidation and he has exhausted his power in giving us the graphic details of the same. It is because of this that the poem becomes at times a bit monotonous. The poem is called one-dimensional and also a mere catalogue of 'lifeless details like wall-paintings'.[6]

However, no body can prescribe his own approach to any theme for the poet. The poet does not have the obligation to go to a place of religious significance 'to kneel and pray.' He has the poetic licence of his own interpretation. Even if we concede that the irreverent and unsympathetic attitude of the protagonist sometimes becomes almost cynical, to dismiss a poem like *Jejuri* as something designed mainly for the amusement of foreign readers is rather hasty and unfair.

It is obvious that the narrator goes to Jejuri "not as a seeker... not as a pilgrim.... He is a kind of traveller...a tourist."[7] Such an approach calls for detachment and complete objectivity which is there in *Jejuri* in so disturbing a manner. The protagonist has no fascination for gods. He is rather much attracted towards the coexistence of innumerable insignificant creatures found in *Jejuri*. He is not a singer of the glorious past. He does not harp on the bygone splendor of yore. There is a deliberate denial of the past and there is a commendable effort to come to grips with the present; no matter, how murky and bleak the present is. It is this quest, which seems to be the cardinal characteristic of Arun Kolatkar's *Jejuri*. His other poems also voice more or less the same feelings. Often his presentation of the priest who is waiting for the bus and thinking: "will there be a puran-poli in his plate?" is misinterpreted as an example of Kolatkar's dry sarcasm. Here, the priest is aspiring for something which is missing from his life. The latent pathos in this poem is often missed. Same is the case with the old woman who 'grabs/ hold of your sleeve/ and tags along' because 'what else can an old woman do/ on hills as wretched as these?' Kolatkar's awareness of the present is acute and he is certainly not among those who lament the loss of heritage. The narrator seems to have believed with J. Krishnamurthi that the past has to be left behind if we want to know the present. In the poem, the shrine gradually takes a back seat. It becomes merely a backdrop for the poet to look beneath the visible reality what may be called the inner reality. It is this quest of inner reality, which makes him celebrate the butterfly: "There is no story behind it.../ it hinges around itself.../ It has no future/ It is pinned down to no past.../ It has taken wretched hills/ under its wings."

However, in a poem in which the alter-ego of the protagonist, i.e. Makarand, a typical modern urban sceptic, says: "take my shirt off/ and go in there to do pooja?/ No thanks/ Not me/ But you go right ahead if that's what you want to do"; one is struck by the absence of a single devout. The old man of the first poem just disappears from the rest of the poems. "When you get off the bus" says the narrator, "You don't step in-side the old man's head." But had he done so, he would have done a great justice to the poem because thereby he could have established patterns of resistance and development between traditional religious faith and modern urban skepticism.

Sri Aurobindo, in his essay on Bankim Chatterjee written in 1894, remarked: "The language which a man speaks and which he has never learned is the language of which he has the nearest sense and in which he expresses himself with greatest fulness, subtlety and power.... To be original in an acquired language is hardly feasible.... It has something unnatural and spurious about it like speaking with a stone in the mouth or walking upon stilts."[8] Clearly, he knew all about the difficulties of creative writing when one's tongue was "in English chains." But he was to concede years later: "It is not true in all cases that one can't write first class things in a learned language. Both in French and English people to whom the language was not native have done remarkable work.... I think, as times goes on people will become more and more polyglot and these mental barriers will begin to disappear."[9] Indeed, they are disappearing very fast and *Jejuri* is an excellent example of it. Despite being a bilingual poet Kolatkar has written *Jejuri* in English because he is not addressing to select readership of a particular province. *Jejuri* is simply a backdrop; it could have been any other place of religious significance, but the concerns of the poet would have remained the same.

Kolatkar seems to have an apathy towards the traditional myths. Strikingly, he exhibits a rare capacity to create myths out of the mundane. A ticket-clerk, the station master, the dish-washer—they all are seen performing their rituals mechanically. The train indicator is "a wooden saint"; the station dog is doing a Buddha—like penance "under/ the tree of arrivals and departures"; the railway timetable is "eight armed"; the young waiter at the tea stall is a 'novice' who has "taken a vow of silence/ when you ask him a question/ he exorcizes you/ by his ablutions in the sink/ and certain ceremonies connected with the washing of cups and saucers."

As the protagonist walks from the temple to the railway station he stops "halfway between/ Jejuri on the one had and the railway station on the other hand" and stands "still like a needle in a trance/ ...that has struck a perfect balance between equal scales/ with nothing left to add or shed." As he stands near a field of jowar he catches sight of 'a dozen cocks and hens' in a kind of 'harvest dance.' These cocks and hens and the butterfly have an energy, a joy and a gusto, a spontaneity and a freedom which is denied to Jejuri and the railway station. The poem ends with the description of the setting sun which is bound to become the rising sun and therefore a symbol of the continuity of life.

In this way, in his *Jejuri*, Arun Kolatkar disclosed surrealistic similarities between an ossified Hindu religious tradition and an equally rigid scientific civilization represented by the railway station. However, the poet celebrates the life force represented by cocks and hens and the butterfly.

NOTES

1. M.K. Naik, "Jejuri: A Thematic Study", *Perspectives on Indian Poetry in English*, ed. M.K. Naik. New Delhi: Abhinav Prakashan, 1984, p. 168.
2. N.P. Acharya, "Jejuri", *Kavi*, Jan. 1978, p. 28. trans. mine.
3. Quoted in Shantinath Desai, "Arun Kolatkaranchi Jejuri: Devanchi vasti" *Pratishthan*, Jan. Feb. 1993, p. 37. trans. Prof. Prakash Chinchore.
4. E.V. Ramakrishnan, "Jejuri, the Search for Place", *Journal of Indian Writing in English*, Jan. 1978, p. 19.

5. Bhalchandra Nemade, "Arun Kolatkar: Dwi-bhashi Kavita", *Teeka Swayamwar.* Bombay: Saket Swayamwar Prakashan, 1990, p. 126. trans. Dr. Chandrakant Deotale.
6. Ravindra Kimbahune, "Jejuri se Arun Kolatkar Tak", *Aaveg*, No. 23, Jan. 1979, p. 61, trans. mine.
7. S.K. Desai, "Arun Kolatkar's *Jejuri*: A House of God", *The Literary Criterion*, XV, 1, 1980, pp. 48-49.
8. Quoted in K.R. Srinivas Iyengar "The Poetry of Sri Aurobindo", *Perspectives on Indian Poetry in English*, ed. M.K. Naik. New Delhi: Abhinav Prakashan, 1984, p. 20.
9. *Ibid.*, p. 21.

10

The Poetic World of Dilip Chitre

Dilip Chitre has been a distinct voice and a distinguished presence both in Marathi and English. He calls himself a 'plurilingual' person and a 'bilingual' poet. Like Arun Kolatkar, Vilas Sarang and Kiran Nagarkar, he also writes both in Marathi and English. Chitre believes that "the voice of poetry cannot be split by the language it does not speak, and the language it chooses to speak excludes no human ear."[1] Born in 1938, Chitre has five collections of poetry in Marathi and three publications in English besides a dozen of books. He is recipient of many awards including Sahitya Akademi Award. His creative genius has found expression not only in his poetry, but also in his novels, short stories, criticism, translations, paintings and film-making. As compared to his Marathi poems which have been published in their entirety, Chitre has published only a small number of his poems in English. But even then his poems have become part of the cannon of modern English poetry and represent him in every major anthology. His three poetical works in English include *Travelling in a Cage* (1980), *The Mountain* (1998), and *No Moon Monday at the River Karha* (2000).

His first collection *Travelling in a Cage* attempts to reveal aspects, situations and languages of the outer and inner worlds, often repressed and hence invisible in the realm of ordinary discourse. It is divided into three sections. The title poem is a sequence of twenty-one poems which centre round the themes of absurdity of life, sense of inescapability, disillusionment, emptiness and futility. The poet here performs his own 'autopsy' and has a feeling of 'sliding down the slopes'. It is an involved, defiant diction with ironic overtones and often with an unmistakable note of bitterness: "...and I was reaching the age of forty/ In the manner one reaches an empty shelf. Where/ Are all of you my dear departed bald ones?/ Angels wearing wigs, gods cleaning dentures?"

Even the vocation of poetry does not offer any succor as the poet is aware that he will leave behind a more 'garbled version' of the same world. He knows that a poem hardly 'upsets the balance of nature' and "the cancer of a lyric/ spreads through nameless lungs." The poet is unable to hide himself as he has no country, no continent to cover his nakedness and travelling without legs or luggage, he finds himself exposed and caged by his own condition. As the very title suggests, the poem charts his existential anguish of which he finds on echo in Ghalib's poem: 'what the cure of this disease was?' This poetic series has shades of death, alienation, fear, dejection and loneliness. It has a touching pathos and also a genuine regret for devoiding things of their names. We come across lines like 'my eyes shed the skin of tears', 'I will injure my lips with the Buddha's smile', 'we have only ourselves to destroy/ And beautiful things to blame'. At the same time, Chitre asks us to decide whether "a man compelled to be silent/ is the same as the man who chooses silence"; thereby asking not only epistemological questions which he keeps asking even today, but the post-cognitive and ontological questions as well. Chitre is against 'excessive' politicization of literary texts and although he feels strongly on various issues, he does not make his poetry an overt vehicle for his socio-political beliefs.

Bombay is a city with which, like many other poets, Chitre also has an ambivalent relationship. In the second section of *Travelling in a Cage*, Chitre's encounter with external world is both complex and interesting. While referring to places, events and friends, the poet confronts the Bombay of porters, beggars, smugglers, politicians, journalists, poets and murderers. The existential pangs of the poet seem to have found in Bombay a sort of objective-correlative and he tells Bombay: "I walk out of murders and riots/ I fall out of smoldering biographies/ I sleep on a bed of burning languages/ sending you up in your essential fire and smoke/ ...once I promised you an epic/ And now you have robbed me/ you have reduced me to rubble/ this concerto ends" ("Ode to Bombay").

In these poems, Bombay is addressed variously: as a city that scatters the mind like a poem, as a garbled relic of someone's empire, as the remaining voice now peopled by estranged millions. This section also has "The Felling of the Bunyan Tree"—a poem that evinces Chitre's ecological concern. As the tree is being killed, "Insects and birds began to leave the tree/ And then they came to its massive trunk/ Fifty men with axes chopped and chopped/ The great tree revealed its rings of two hundred years/ We watched in terror and fascination this slaughter/ As a raw mythology revealed to us its age." Chitre gives this nail a tap further when he says that soon after the removal of the Bunyan tree, they left Baroda to Bombay: "Where there are no trees except the one/ Which grows and seethes in one's dreams, its aerial roots/ Looking for ground to strike".

The poem acquires a new height as the image of the tree links the process of dehumanization with the anguish of the unrealized dreams.

The third section of this collection contains "Ambulance Ride"—a long-brooding poem which contemplates death as it is written on the demise of a dear friend. Vilas Sarang thinks that this kind of poem is "rare in the Indian English realm, where poets prefer a quiet, muted tone".[2] The poem is moving, full of touching pathos and uses the word 'remember' like a refrain—evoking a whole world of memories.

Travelling in a Cage, thus, is remarkable for its tonal variations due to the poet's multi-dimensional engagement with a hydra-headed reality. Despite the facts that the themes are familiar and the poet has not broken any new grounds, he has given here ample testimony of his talent. Some of the poems may rightly be called "high pitched"[3] and the ironic mode, which has been nearly exhausted by Indian poets writing in English, at times gives us a feeling of *deja-vu*, but all our apprehensions regarding yet another predictable poet on the scene are dispelled by Chitre's second poetic sequence *The Mountain* which appeared in 1998. While making his feature film *Godam*, Dilip Chitre wrote these poems like a compulsive personal journal. He was close to death on location at Navli Village (Near Jejuri) and these poems mirror the yearnings of a man who has seen the face of death. The long gap of 18 years after his first collection has done a lot of good to his poetry as that initial streak to shock, mock and jeer has given way to pensive reflection. The poem rehabilitates God in the context of modern Indian poetry in English. While writing these poems, the poet was undergoing increasing desperation and a deepening crisis. The landscape of Navli and its ethos have played a great role in shaping the creative process of the poet. In these poems, the poet pushes himself over the edge, falls into the abyss, and mysteriously finds himself at the top of the mountain, serenely surveying the significance of human life: "I am here to see/ what others do not/ to hear/ what others can not/ to touch what any body can/ but no one cares to feel/ to taste/ what perishes/ to smell/ the withering events of life/ and to preserve it all and to/ even go on adding tender wrinkles inside a stone head" ("Witness"). *The Mountain* is one man's surreal quest for the eternal. The poet is not a devotee and yet he feels himself chosen by God and this makes him feel that because he is driven by a divine madness, he is attracting malice from the ambitious, evoking terror among the weak and creating confusion among the clever. "So the world saw in me/ A suicidal drunk/ A promiscuous lunatic/ An obsessive fool/ A wounded lover/ Anything but a man blessed by you/ Driven by you alone/ Given gifts no one can rob/ In the midst of disasters" ("It was Then that I Realized"). Dilip Chitre's God weeps for his devotees with eyes of stone when he watches the pilgrims entering their 'own ant-hills'. A weeping God, in his poetic conception, crosses joys and sorrows and enters "the strange area/ of morning beyond the mountain." The surreal delineation of this metaphysical quest lends these poems a distinct charm. As the experience itself is complex and defies a transparent articulation, the poetic idiom tends to be cryptic and abstruse. This is not detrimental in appreciating the poem, as it successfully keeps the inherent invitation of the poem intact.

No Moon Monday at the River Karha is the latest poetic series of Chitre. It is precipitated by the Somvati Amavasya festival at the River Karha near Jejuri which is supposed to be the capital of king Khandoba—a terrestrial incarnation of the pre-vedic deity Rudra or Shiva. Somvati Amavasya is celebrated on every New Moon day that occurs on a Monday. The poet has attended this festival several times and has always experienced a "profound cathartic effect"[4] on himself. Though the poem has a specific date—March 6, 2000—when the poet had visited the same festival in the company of his German poet-writer-artist friend, it is not drawn out of him by that one festival. Chitre believes:

> poems wait to happen. Given time, they unfold. Often, they need a trigger, a catalyst, a push. Sometimes, if not always, they surprise you by gathering so much that has been suppressed or shoved aside year after year and denied the space to become a complete event drawing into its vortex forces of incomplete but potent experience: all the imaginable yet elusive elements that await their moment of realized fusion.[5]

This series which has seven poems, seems to be an extension of *The Mountain*, though the connection between the two poems is neither linear nor chronological. They, according to the poet, are parts of a 'seamless single event' hidden in his psyche. Like *The Mountain*, this poem also begins with a quest for self-identity in the wake of the festival. Thousands of pilgrims have thronged to witness Khandoba and the poet wonders whether he is a participant, an outsider who observes to report to other outsiders, a tourist guide or a dissertationist. Here pilgrimage is an open narrative in which everything tells different stories. It is apparent that here Chitre is in Arun Kolatkar's territory; but nevertheless he is treading an untrodden path. There is an inevitable intertextuality between the two poems. Both are quest poems, but of different kinds. Kolatkar's *Jejuri* is full of the pictures of aridity, ugliness, decay, neglect, fossilization and perversion. It has been criticized for being "not so much a poem of discovery as the proverbial drain-inspector's poetic reportage."[6] Though Chitre defends his poet friend Kolatkar, his own encounter with the same place does not inspire him to debunk it; rather the landscape as well as the gathering of thousands of pilgrims provide him a space for introspection and self-exploration. While reading *The Mountain* and *No Moon...* one has to keep in mind that Chitre has translated from traditional Marathi mystical and religious poetry including the 1311-century poem "Anubhavamrut" ("The Immortal Experience of Being") by Shri Jnandev and also from the 17th-century poet-saint Tukaram. Chitre has travelled extensively and his global vision seems to have reinforced his nativity. His poetry abounds in the references of these saints and their poems and this makes it distinguished from other modern poets in English. Both these poems give well-grounded proof of his vital link with seven centuries of Bhakti poetry in Marathi and its pan-Indian ethos. He says: "I have learnt the secret/ of integrity/ the bhakta is the Lord/ In his moment of loneliness" (*The Mountain*). Mingled with his surreal imagination these poems are non-atavistic as they attempt to transcend. In the fifth poem of this series, the poet tells us of a possessed woman who is dancing beside herself in a trance and he thinks of her as 'the splendor of every incarnate passion'. When she falls to the ground in utter exhaustion—the poet feels: "I was the belittled one/ who would go back to the city/ with an image/ That would haunt forever/ The man who dared not enter the magic circle/ of her act of passionate transcendence/ can I betray my own experience/ To write a poem after this." At this point, he recalls his own moments of transcendence. He says: "Dilip Chitre died here on a No Moon Monday/ In a cloud of turmeric dust" and has crossed "the frontier of all songs." His poetry is an awakened voice which is—

> ...not about light but the lightness of one's last breath. This is not about the dark but the moment of seeing it all. This is not about death but the memory of the beginning. Or the beginning of memory and structured time.

The poems like "The Mountain" and "No Moon..." are focussed on the process of transcendence, "the continuous crisis of being that sucks in everything in its field."[7] There is a certain elusive quality in these poems which resists the reader's complacency and he is compelled to return to them, spellbound by their composite experience that refuses to be reduced in stock-generalizations. The multi-directional movement of these poems encompasses faith, sexuality, love and transcendence—all together in a complex structure. His poetry explores tradition with a modern consciousness and renders the classifications and compartmentalizations like tradition, modernity and contemporaneity as pathetic. It imposes new patterns of language, reflection, vision and imagination on its readers. The dark interior of the earlier poems is irradiated by a spiritual illumination in his later poetry. There is a steady progression in the poetic world of Dilip Chitre—from the darkness towards light. That is why the poet says:

> This is no mountain
> This is light itself
> And I am the fool
> who dares to climb it.
>
> ("A Poet's Task"—*The Mountain*)

NOTES

1. Dilip Chitre, "Afterword", *The Mountain*. Pune: Vijaya Chitre, 1998, p. 44.
2. Vilas Sarang, "Introduction", *Indian English Poetry Since 1950: An Anthology*, ed. Vilas Sarang. Bombay: Orient Longman, 1990, p. 37.
3. *Idem*.
4. Dilip Chitre, "Forward", *No Moon Monday at the River Karha*. Pune: Vijaya Chitre, 2000, p. 3.
5. *Idem*.
6. K.R. Srinivas Iyengar, "Post Script", *Indian Writing in English*. New Delhi: Sterling Publishers, 1962; sixth edition 1987, p. 723.
7. Dilip Chitre, "Forward", *No Moon Monday at the River Karha*. Pune: Vijaya Chitre, 2000, p. 3.

11

The Science Fiction of Satyajit Ray and Jayant V. Narlikar—A Comparative Look

The debate still goes on whether science fiction is a part of serious literature but its popularity across the globe is unquestioned and undeniable. A science fiction writer is a kind of visionary, a futurist and his prophetic prowess compels us to see not only between but also beyond his lines for there might be lurking the shadows of near or distant future. He is wont to envisage the most uncanny, bizarre and even apparently absurd inventions, weapons, conflicts and clashes in this world and beyond and portrays them in such a convincing manner that everything seems plausible and possible and while going through it we are more than willing to suspend our disbelief. Written in 1816 by Mary Shelley, *Frankenstein* becomes an allegory for the self-destructive side of science and its protagonist passes into an idiom for creating the tool of one's own destruction. Jules Verne made a prediction about the journey to the moon that came to be true in 1969 with Armstrong's landing on the moon. H.G. Wells introduces his marvellous inventions and daring adventures that continue to excite us even today. Huxley, Orwell and Stapledon, with their futuristic vision gave a new direction to science fiction which was carried further by Brian Aldiss, Issac Asimov, Ray Bradbury, Octavia Butler, Arthur C. Clarke, Robert A. Heinlein, Ursula K. Leguin, Gene Rodenbury, Fred Hoyle and many more.

But when we look for their Indian counterparts, we are a little disappointed. Science fiction, though quite popular in the mediums like T.V. and films, has not found many practitioners here. The reasons are many and varied. Ancient India was remarkable for its rapid strides in the field of science. A land of Charak, Sushrut, Bhaskar, Aryabhatta, Varahmihir and many others, India's cultural continuity suffered a rupture due to foreign invasions and the fruits of modern science came to it through the West. Our mythology is such an incredible mix of fantasy, science, moral education, spiritualism, and is so all inclusive that probably we never felt any need for the kind of fiction that anticipates the invasion of Earth by Martians or by the creatures inhabiting some other planet. We have our own Yakshas, Gandharvas, Kinnars, Rakshasas, Gods of every hue and shape and size taking care of all walks of human life; therefore this extremely rich, varigated and colourful Indian imagination leaves little scope for genres like science fiction to thrive. Moreover, the curse of illiteracy also is responsible to a large extent, for the paucity of Indian science fiction writers who can be counted on fingers. Especially, science fiction has been popular in Bangla and Marathi literature and this paper concerns itself with two most outstanding writers—Satyajit Ray and Jayant Vishnu Narlikar.

Satyajit Ray is very much like our own Da Vinci—he is a writer, editor, poet, film-maker, illustrator, and what not. This multi-faceted genius has created Professor Shonku—an extraordinary scientist and inventor whose amazing inventions never fail to amuse and surprise us. Shonku's first story "The Astronaut's Diary" appeared in 1961 and up to 1992 nearly 38 stories published in eight-story collections. His full name is Trilokeshwar Shonku and he lives in Giridih with a male servant and a pet cat 'Newton'. Having completed his graduation with honours in both Physics and Chemistry when 20 years old, Shonku dedicated himself to his inventions after a brief stint of teaching. Bald, bespectacled and bearded—Professor Shonku is almost a global figure who frequently travels all over the world and works in collaboration with scientists of various countries. He is a polyglot who knows 69 languages.

Satyajit Ray uses the form of diary to record the exploits of Shonku who can be ranked next only to Edison as far as his incredible inventions are concerned. Ray, who received science education only up to high school level, had such a remarkable gift of imagination that nearly 38 inventions of Shonku are forever etched in the memory of Shonku readers. The list of inventions includes a snuff gun—which, when fired at someone's nose, makes people sneeze for hours together; a rocket—in which Shonku flew off on his final journey to Mars and then to Tafa; Miracureall—the miraculous medicine which cured all kinds of ailments except common cold; Mangorange—a hybrid fruit which is a mixture of mango and orange; carbothin—an electricity resisting fabric which can be used to make garments; Microsonograph—sound amplifier which allows us to hear even the most inaudible noise as made by ants or screams of a flower when it is plucked; Robu—his robot who has the additional knowledge of Maths and with Shonku's scientist friend Rudolf Palmer's efforts develops the faculty of sensing Shonku's feelings; Annihilin Pistol—as Shonku dislikes bloodshed he invented it to merely annihilate his enemy. Professor Shonku is pitted against the best minds in the field of science across the world and earns not only their admiration and cooperation, but also incurs jealousy and hostility from some of them—which contributes to his adventures an element of thrill and suspense. Probably, except South Asian countries, Shonku has been to all parts of the world in the course of his exploits. Ray very adroitly incorporates bits of knowledgeable information about these exotic places which helps to make his narrative more convincing. Shonku has been to Egypt, Sweden, Norway, Hong Kong, Heidelberg, Bagdad, Switzerland, Chile, Spain, Osaka, Africa, China, Italy, London and his scientist friends, in different parts of the world, help him by their specialization in various branches of science. The character of Abinash Babu who is Shonku's neighbour lends an occasional touch of humour to these Shonku tales. He appears acrimonius at first but gradually serves as a foil to Shonku. He has no appreciation for Shonku's scientific genius and he cares little for his research or inventions. Yet, we find a development in their relationship over the course of different stories as Shonku develops a tolerance for him. His sense of humour provides a welcome relief in these thrilling adventures. Another character who is introduced much later in these stories is Nokur Chandra Biswas who has the powers of hypnotism, telepathy and clairvoyance. He helps Shonku in the perilous situations and warns him beforehand of impending danger. Shonku also reciprocates his kindness and friendly help. He loves his cat Newton so much that he invents Marjarin, a medicine for the longivity of the cat and in his last story the cat is 24 years old.

A "mild-mannered" incarnation of Arthur Conan Doyle's Professor Challanger, Professor Shonku is a man of principles, courage and integrity. His sympathy for the underprivileged, his indifference to money-making, his stand against the wrong makes him a distinguished figure in Indian science fiction. Besides Shonku, in the sixties, Ray had written a story "Bonkubabu's Friend" in which he presented his initial drawing for Extra Terristrial. A space ship lands on a village and the alien helps a simpleton clerk Bonkubabu who is transformed from a timid, diffident man into a self-asserting individual who can call a spade a spade. Prior to this, the aliens in the science fiction are traditionally portrayed as inimical and hostile to the inhabitants of the Earth. It was Ray's innovative concept to present them as friendly and helpful to the human beings. Based on this story Ray's script *The Alien* was to be made in a Hollywood movie but for a number of reasons, the project could not take off. Its re-emergence as Spielberg's 'E.T.' caused great controversy as Ray fans accused Spielberg of plagiarism—a charge that he denied. But Ray himself has claimed that "E.T. would not have been possible without my script of *The Alien* being available throughout America in mimeographed copies".[1]

If Satyajit Ray has thrilled and entertained us with his Professor Shonku stories in Bangla, Jayant Vishnu Narlikar, in Marathi has done pioneer work in popularising science through his science fiction. Unlike Ray, Narlikar who is Indian astrophysicist and cosmologist of international repute, has not written a series of stories featuring a single character. His stories deal with some kind of a crisis forewarned by the present indications which are obvious yet ignored. In one of his interviews, when Ashok Mahadevan asked him if reads much of science fiction as he himself writes it, he replied—"Not much, because I am turned off if the fiction contradicts the science I know without explanations. For example, relativity says that nothing can move faster than light, but in one novel people were traversing the galaxy in the matter of a few years whereas light would take a hundred thousand years."[2] Narlikar's science fiction respects the scientific parameters as paramount and he is not in favour of taking liberties to make his work sensational. He has written a number of short stories and novels including *The Cosmic Explosion* and *The Adventure*. His novel *Return of Vaman* is a mix of science and astrology and also provides us a telling look at beaurocracy, international espionage and smuggling. One of his reasons for writing science fiction is his desire to share the excitement of working in astronomy with a lay person and in this direction, he was inspired by his mentor Sir Fred Hoyle, astrophysicist and well-known writer of science fiction. A further reason is that "Science could also be made less intimidating to many of us if it is in the form of science fiction stories or novels."[3] His book *Tales of the Future* exemplifies this. It includes his ten short stories. His story "The Ice Age Cometh" centres round the prediction of Bombay scientist Vasant Chitnis about the arrival of the Ice Age. The world's best scientist ridicule this prognostication but when the city of Bombay experiences snowfall and the country is gripped by a severe cold wave, the realisation dawns on the scientist community that the prediction has come true. At last, Chitnis again comes to rescue and invents a way to overcome the ice. "The Death of a Megapolice" forbodes the death of Bombay on October 10, 2041 as the metro is consumed by an inferno. Reviewing this story for *The Tribune*, Aditya Rishi links the torrential rains that flooded Mumbai in 2005 with this foreboding and relates Narlikar to New-age Nostradamus in prophesying the end of the city.[4]

But perhaps Narlikar's real achievement, in his short stories is "The Rare Idol of Ganesha", Pramod Rangnekar, India's right-arm bowler dramatically turns into left-arm bowler by a scientist. When he comes on the field again, in his career's final test, he makes the England batting order crumble that does not know how to respond to his unfamiliar bowling and is all out for just 78 runs. Rangnekar disappears after the test match and is found the next day in Police station with the memory of match erased from his mind. Like Ray, Narlikar's protagonist is also a scientist in his fiction, but unlike him, Narlikar insists upon choosing an Indian locale instead of the most exotic places in the world. His endevour is to make his readers identify with the locale, characters and situations that he portrays in his science fiction. The scientist characters used by Ray and Narlikar are divested of their immediate families. There is no mention of their wives or children. They appear to be happily single and can afford to go on with their worship of science without distractions. Their Robots are not lifeless automatons; they are given a distinct personality and individuality. Both Ray and Narlikar evince concerns that are human and they employ science fiction as a vehicle to project the possibilities as well as threats before society. Whereas Ray amuses us with Shonku's amazing inventions and thrills us by contriving perilous situations for him, Narlikar focusses on sound scientific superstructure for his science fiction which is enlivened by the local flavour and an occassional skilful interweaving of Indian mythology. Ray is a master storyteller who creates a rivetting tale using science as a backdrop; Narlikar is a renowned scientist whose thrust remains on the possible culmination of the actual present situations. He gives greater importance to the scientific over the literary aspects; Ray, on the other hand, seems to create a parallel science-world in which we imagine a scientist whose laboratory would be full of chemicals such as bicarbonic acid, paradoxite powder, carbodiabolic acid, nitroannihilin acid and phorosotonic acid. Obviously, the backdrop of science that Ray chooses to create is virtual, not actual, his objective being the curiosity and amusement of his reader. To achieve this, he peoples the world of Shonku with interesting characters like his servant Prahlad who is dimwit but loyal and Abinash Babu—funny but a kind soul. Narlikar, like a light rope-walker walks the edge between science and fiction and while striving to make his fiction engaging, he refuses to sacrifice the science which serves as the backbone to his fictional anatomy. Narlikar gives due importance to the social commitment of science fiction writer and his science fiction exemplifies this. In 1970s, he wrote a story about the possibility of knowing the sex of the unborn child which has assumed horrible dimensions in the present times. Also, in 1976, he had written a story on the possibility of a comet approaching the Earth on a trajectory that would lead to a head-on collision. To save Earth from such a catastrophe, scientists successfully launch a spaceship with a nuclear device that explodes near the comet, changing its trajectory. In the late 1980s NASA was seriously considering an action of this kind in a similar situation. Today a spacewatch mission is operative to preclude any such situation. This is how genuine science fiction envisages the future and anticipates real situations. Critics like Debjani Sengupta who casually compares Bengali and Marathi science fiction and in this context quotes Hans Harder's words to denigrate Marathi science fiction as "sterlised and remystified",[5] should reconsider their views in the light of Narlikar's fiction that sincerely attempts to inculcate a scientific temper in its readers and, in his best work, strikes an almost perfect balance between science and fiction. And while doing so, social concerns are never out of focus for him. He says, "I would like the sci-fi literature to be also conscious of the science-society interaction. Thus, there are issues like stem cells research, cloning, etc. in biology, researches into nuclear devices, and the spying capability of remote sensing satellites, which raise moral and social questions."[6]

One charge can be levelled against both Ray and Narlikar that their fiction primarily appeals to the young minds, but then it is a charge that has always been levelled against the very genre of science fiction itself. The popularity of the science fiction of Ray and Narlikar bears testimony to the fact that readers, irrespective of their age, relish to cater this eternal juvenile craving for watching with fascination how the improbable turns into possible. The science fiction of Satyajit Ray and Jayant V. Narlikar is the kind of science fiction which is created when the objectivity of science interacts with the creativity of imagination within an ambience of genuine social concerns. It is not only captivating and engrossing; it is also enlightening and illuminating; it does not simply amuse, thrill and entertain us; it also forewarns and wakes us up to the potential threats.

NOTES

1. http://www.indiasta.com/satyajitray.html
2. http://www.rd-india.com/newsite/other/facetoface_jun07.asp
3. Murli N. Krishnaswamy, "Science Fiction with a Local Flavour". *The Hindu*, Aug. 09, 2005.
4. Aditya Rishi, "The Faraway World", *The Tribune*, Aug. 28, 2005.
5. http://www.sarai.net/publications/readers/03-shaping-technologies
6. Jayant V. Narlikar, "The Role of Science Fiction in the Present Age of Science", *Dream 2047*, Vol. 9, No. 3, Dec. 2006, p. 38.

12

Society as a Self-replicating Ensemble in *Evam Indrajit*

Recipient of several awards including prestigious Sangeet Natak Akademi award for playwriting in 1968, Badal Sircar is one of the most representative voices of the modern post-independence theatre. Badal Sircar's play *Evam Indrajit* has been considered as a pioneer play in the modern, experimental Indian theatre. Originally written in Bangla, the play has been translated into many Indian regional languages as well as in English. Also, it has been successfully staged all over India and is widely acclaimed.

Evam Indrajit tries to convey a realistic theme in an experimental manner. The play does not have a linear narrative. It rather can be called a collage of the various fragments and facets of contemporary life with its characteristic repetitiveness. Despite lacking in episodic interest, the play captivates our interest as it deals with the issues directly related to the kind of life we live. The cyclical structure of the play conveys the monotony of a mechanical existence. At times, the dialogues are broken, repetitive, even absurd—signifying the element of *déjà vu* prevalent in the life we choose to live. The play begins with a writer who is looking for proper subject for his play. But he is in a fix as the kind of people he would like to write about lack the 'drama' in their lives. They are Amal, Vimal and Kamal. Indrajit wants to be different but is incapable of being so under the crushing pressures of a society where conformity is regarded as supreme virtue. Thus, the play revolves round the plight of modern people who keep on replicating each other's lives with neither potential nor desire for any originality in them. Generations after generations keep imitating the same mode of existence without much change. Amal, Vimal and Kamal represent these stereotypes. The play's title *Evam Indrajit* is very significant as Indrajit tries to explore the ways to veer away from the common rut. He refuses to be Nirmal—just another clone of Amal, Vimal and Kamal. The play does not celebrate Indrajit's success in becoming Indrajit; but it underlines his choice for carving a different identity. Adherence to the prescribed roles scripted by the society, mimicking the ways, modes, values and even the dull, hackneyed conversation of each other laced with oft-repeated, insufferably threadbare comments, echoing a predictable, routine, mundane, monotonous and meaningless life; or striving to have a distinct individual entity, discarding the so-called security and safety of a conformist social structure, is a choice that is fraught with risks and perils of getting perished under the giant wheel of the same society. Badal Sircar does not seek easy solutions by creating a hero; he rather prefers to point at the enormous obstacles in the way—the traditional mindset, the quest for security and certainty in a highly volatile world, the pull back of societal forces, and the irresolvable inner conflicts. Says the writer summarizing the human situation:

> Amal retires. His son Amal takes up a job. Vimal is ill. His son Vimal takes up a job. Kamal is dead. His son Kamal takes up a job. And Indrajit. And Indrajit's son Indrajit. There on the pavement is a seven-year-old boy with a box in his hand and a baby in his arms. There, on the pavement near him is a woman. Her name is Leela. Her husband died of TB. Beyond there is an orange sky under which Manasi wants to love life. Life. So many loves. So many parts and bits and parcels and pieces and molecules and atoms and they mix and mingle and move and turn and go round and round till they become a giant ferries wheel. And I have to write about them. I have to put into language the drama of these atoms going round and round. But language is senile and words are battered and maimed. (221-22)

The character of writer acts as the connecting thread—the *sutradhar*—who himself seems to be an extension of Indrajit in the quest of his own identity. Both of them have made a difficult choice but they realize that their success lies not in reaching their destination but in treading the path towards it. Whether they will ever be able to reach there holds little relevance. Thus, the play shows an optimistic leaning despite the apparent failure of the protagonist. The path and the journey assume greater significance than the final destination:

> And hence/ There's no end./ There's no hope/ Of fulfillment/ By the holy shrine/ At journey's end./ Forget the questions/ Forget the grief,/ And have faith/ In the road./ No shrine for us/ No God for us/ But the road,/ The endless road. (250)

G.P. Deshpande has aptly noted that Badal Sircar "introduced a new dramatic idiom." He further remarks that "*Evam Indrajit* is a classic of contemporary Indian theatre" (xvix). It is a fact that Badal Sircar changed the concerns of modern drama and introduced a language which was refreshingly different from the stagnant prose that dominated Indian theatre writing for well over a century. *Evam Indrajit* is a play without a plot and yet it presents a generation before us through amazing economy of words. Stylistically, it chooses to employ the refrain, the incantatory tone of counting the numbers—forwards and backwards, and names; also poetry to articulate the abstraction so unavoidably entrenched in a theme that has the magnitude of dealing with the maladies afflicting a whole society, an entire nation.

Badal Sircar dispenses with a large cast of characters, assigning different roles to the same actors. Also, he uses minimal property in this play and provides ample opportunity to the enthusiastic play-directors for experimenting further and improvise. His technique of involving the audience is also in consonance with the theme of the play that deals with the masses. In the early sixties, all these innovative techniques remarkably contributed in ushering in a new era in the theatre movement of India. Despite the fact that we have come a long way since the times the play had been written, it retains its appeal through the power of the quintessentially pertinent questions it raises that keep confronting us perennially.

REFERENCE

Sircar, Badal. *Evam Indrajit*. trans. Girish Karnad. *Modern Indian Drama—An Anthology*, ed. G.P. Deshpande, New Delhi: Sahitya Akedemi, 2000; rpt. 2015. Print.

13

A Critical Appraisal of the Short Stories of Krishna Baldev Vaid

In Krishna Baldev Vaid, one is faced with a short-story writer who has very well understood the complex stresses of modern times and therefore his short stories have a form of their own. A conscious formlessness in the shape of experimental writing can be seen everywhere in his stories. His stories read like a poem in their intensity and lyrical description. Born in 1927 in western Punjab, now part of Pakistan, Krishna Baldev Vaid lived through harrowing experiences in refugee camps and trains during the carnage that accompanied the Partition of India. Strangely enough this most traumatic and central experience of his life has hardly found expression in his stories. Rather, his world is located in the corridors of human consciousness. Educated at Punjab and Harvard Universities, Vaid has taught English and American Literature in India and abroad. A bilingual he has published over twenty-five books in Hindi and English. Two of his novels, two collections of short stories and a book on the technique in tales of Henry James are published in English to critical acclaim.

Vaid is a writer who builds symbolic structures to convey through the use of the terrible, piercing irony his view of man's pathetic nakedness in the face of the crumbling edifice of a civilization gone mad. He is obsessively concerned with the dark, uncannily oppressive inner recesses of his intensely introvert characters. His stories, by and large, are not crowded thorough-fares of action and conflict. He records the reactions and ruminations of his characters, etching the contours of the interior landscape of the individual's mind. Take for example, Amina in "Silence" who "carries about her a flavor of unhappiness which seems to be the essence of the pain of living."[1] This story reveals the enviable grasp of the medium and a highly imaginative faculty. There are two couples—one is married, the other is about to be married. There is the house without any sign of domesticity and there is silence—silence or years which the protagonist wants to thaw but every effort is followed by a fresh layer. Towards the end of the story this silence supervenes—one marriage goes on the rocks, the other never takes place.

As a story writer, Vaid loves to break bounds and shuns the beaten track. He has penchant for the unusual and teratoid. We are bewildered by the startling confessions, bizarre situations, the unpredictable nuances, nightmarish experiences, half-hearted justifications and a series of contradictions. The imaginary forays of his protagonists into a world of trampled desires, fading smiles, weird conjectures and dried-up longings are conveyed with great power. "There is a narrow dungeon in my house. It is cluttered with all kinds of junk 'I have saved' all my life and forgotten about. And it is also cluttered with darkness—the useless darkness I have saved all my life and forgotten about, as well as 'the useless darkness' that oozes out of everyday that passes. The door of this dungeon emits darkness and swallows it simultaneously" (139).

The perennial search for perfection and peace and the desperate efforts to get ever the haunting sense of desolation and failure which culminates into coming to terms with reality so far discarded, is the basic theme of Vaid's stories. The protagonist in "An Evensong" says, "...I start licking the salt of my failures, it is like an animal licking its sores: I like unsuccessful people, they are my kin: they have a special odor: I hate the greasiness of success. I believe that every success is ill-gotten.... I do not get any peace from this belief. I have doubts about its truth..." (150).

The frantic attempts at self-delusion and the bitter realization of the futility of such attempts is the ever-recurring theme of the short stories of Vaid, treated with morbid candor, wild imagination, a generous dose of black humor, sweeping irony, intellectual suppleness and comic absurdity. The agonized quest for peace is reflected in a number of stories. "The Fourth Window" end in this way:

> The sights I see through the first window give me pain as well as pleasure: the sights through the second only revulsion the sights through the third only dread.

I do not know when and how the fourth window will open and on what sights. I do not know how to open lit. My blind faith says it will open some evening of itself in answer to the mute entreaties of my lacerated hands. And that it will open on nothing, nothing at all. And after I have had a glimpse of that void, I shall be released from this room.

These days I spend every evening waiting for the release (144).

In these stories, we often find a streak of self-derison on the part of the Protagonists. In "The Old Man in the Park" he thinks that he looks like "a bearded effigy made of dried-up longings or perhaps like some dream of a mad man." His characters often trample themselves. For example, the narrator in "My Effigy" says. "I've begun to despise myself. My body seems alien to me, my mind a mess—I've become my effigy, battered and bruised, covered with spit, pierced by curses" (138). Sometimes this self-derision reaches to the extent of self-floggelation. Acutely aware of his miserable state, the protagonist in "An Evensong" echoing the feelings of most of Vaid's characters, says: "I am one of those absolute failures who cherish no illusions, give themselves no concession, give others no concession, draw no satisfaction from any success; every evening I drink steadily until it begins to throb; when it does, I burst into a monologues... after that point I fall asleep or perhaps pass out; one of these days I shall pass away after that point, I do not draw any satisfaction from it" (150).

More often than not, in the stories of Vaid, the protagonist encounters a character who serves as his alter-ego. In fact, this character is a shadow of himself; an extension of his own psyche, and is always shrouded in ambiguity. This enables him to divine the mind of the protagonists.

Towards the end of the story, this character slowly fades out, leaving behind the narrator who tries to "draw some solace from the fact that nobody comes into this room, that nobody goes out of it—nobody, that is, except me—that the thief does not exist, that he is a figment of my imagination. But even this thought does not give me any permanent peace of mind" (150). In "My Effigy", he makes a suggestion to his wife to get an effigy of himself so that she can keep hitting at it, to provide her a release for all her fury and she does the same. She is very happy now, at peace with herself and her husband, all sweetness and light, bursting with zest for life but the hero is absolutely deflated because he himself has become his effigy. The old man says: "On some midnights and fierce noon, when I am slouching around like a self-respecting two-legged insect, a shadow appears and starts slouching along with me, whispering incoherently to me about those huge questions. I think that shadow is my only true companion now" (169).

Satire is an effective tool in the hands of Vaid. In his world the comic absurdity is inextricably linked up with social criticism. It does not aim at laughter; it strikes us with the full force and leaves us stunned. The rag-picker girl, ironically named Bhookh Kumari in the story "An Evening with Bhookh Kumari" says:

> People have acquired heaps of black money, that's why the rubbish heaps are rich. My mother used to bless the municipality for not removing rubbish regularly.
>
> My mother collected quite a dowry for me entirely from the rubbish heaps. You need not pity us. I look upon my work as a form of art. You write, "I pick rubbish". (162-63)

The writer who is writing a story on "Hunger" is not able to accept this girl's offer to live in a shanty, take off his fancy clothes and wear rugs, sleep by the side of an open drain and go back to his youth when he used to know hunger from personal experience and dreamt of abolishing it.

Though in most of his stories Vaid is preoccupied with the exploration of the emotional ecology of the turbulent world of individuals, his theme are of surprising variety. "The Stone of a Jamun" is remarkable exposition of the exploitation of two little children by the ruthless Jamun-seller who makes a false promise to give them some (Jamun) and uses them for the sell without keeping it. Vaid has an uncanny eye for details and his descriptions of the heat, the deserted bus stand, the dark, glistening Jamuns, the hungry stare of the little boy, the integrity of the elder boy and the helplessness and disgust of the narrator are memorable for vividness. The story is spiced with a colourfully meaningful selection of details: "The Jamun-seller was busy shaping his pyramids into purple perfection, the little boy's brother too had started staring at the brat's mouths and moving his mouth over his imaginary Jamuns. The two brothers opened and shut their mouths more or less simultaneously they swallowed their saliva as if it was Jamun juice" (132-33).

But the narrator does not have money to buy Jamuns for boys. He hopes that they would start cursing the Jamun-seller. He intends to support them if they speak for themselves. But they just cry with their hands out and still urge the Jamun-seller to give them some. The narrator is annoyed and so are we because of this unexpected breakdown of the elder boy. Vaid does not stop here, he gives the nail a final tap and concludes—"Then I saw that the little boy had started picking up the stones of the Jamuns. Before I boarded my bus I heard one of the customers saying to his companion—Jamun is a wonderful fruit, you know, even the stone of a Jamun is good; it is the best remedy for impotence" (133).

It is this way that Vaid sees life's significant aspects behind an apparently trivial incident or an event which others are prone to pass by indifferently. He makes a memorable story out of a normal roadside scene. Such indelible glimpses of life are the stuff of which his stories are made.

Generally, in the form of monologues, his stories also manifest his mastery over dialogues. There are generally no plots and the terrifying images of the modern man's nightmarish condition are conveyed in a style that is lucid, succinct and riveting. Some stories are very short but they are complete in themselves. Vaid resists in indulging anything that is superfluous. From the beginning to the end, without missing the smallest details and without overstretching anything, he creates memorable stories. His prose is powerful and evocative and he often soars high above into flights of fancy like a typical poet.

However, there is an element of bitterness clearly perceptible when he deals with marital life. Also, he has a tendency to shock the reader with the situations and characters. Quite often his characters confess their perverse pleasure. Sometimes, he strays far in his fantasy and the reader finds it difficult to keep pace with him. But all these do not detract from his worth as a significant writer of considerable intrinsic merit. His stories are remarkable for the felicity of expression, his capacity for clear and realistic portrayal, ingenuity, compression and originality with a strong admixture of fantasy.

NOTE

1. Krishna Baldev Vaid, *Dying Alone and Ten Short Stories.* New Delhi, Penguin Books India Pvt. Ltd., 1992, p. 117. Subsequent page numbers are given within the text after quotes.

14

Meena Alexander's *Nampally Road*: An Expedition to the 'Self'

Mary Elizabeth, often hailed as Meena Alexander, is the finest artist of the South-Asian Diasporas' aesthetics. As an author, she plunges deep into the ocean of quest for women's identity and concerns the issues of displacement and alienation of immigrants. Born in India, dwelled in Sudan, pursued her doctorate degree in Britain's Nottingham University, a subsequent return to India and then establishing herself in New York—exhibits a pattern of multiple dislodgements and pull ups, that naturally fragmented her identity so much so that it is arduous to track down her bona fide 'self' on this planet, and compels her to say, "I am a woman cracked by multiple migrations. Uprooted so many times I can connect nothing with nothing" (*FL* 03). Her novel *Nampally Road* is a paradigm of such expedition in the wrap of contemporary woman and central character of the book. In fact, rightly puts Githa Hariharan, "*Nampally Road* is the landscape Alexander's young protagonist, Mira Kannadical, must negotiate on a quest that involves personal as well as political challenges, choices and discoveries" (Foreword).

A step forward to the decades-old ideology of the feminist writer, Simon de Beauvoir in her work *The Second Sex* that, "One is not born but rather becomes a woman...it is civilization as a whole that produces this creature...which is described as Feminine" (10); Meena Alexander harbingers the notion that—it is female body that possesses the strength to bring a life into existence, who knows the implications to bear a child in its womb for months and to experience suffering to give birth to an offspring. Yet, it is women who has to wear a 'Sari' a metaphor of shackles and fetters that confines her, and treated as an inferior sex curbed down to conventional roles.

Alexander's universe chronicles the 'place' of woman in the current aeon, which is no less abysmal as it used to be centuries ago. It is the bitter truth that woman has been inflicted innumerable torments and pains, attributable to its treatment as an oppressed sect of human being. Undeniably, a woman has been silenced from the dawn of civilization by the patriarchal structure of society. Irrefutably, thus, a woman as a member of Diaspora is subjected to dual marginalization, first as an immigrant and then as a subaltern.

The writer's fabrication of the novel *Nampally Road*, exhibits a protagonist, Mira Kannadical, who returns to Hyderabad after accomplishing her Ph.D. from England, building castles in the air that it would be a country where her aspirations and expectations would reach their zenith. But soon after, on her arrival in the country, she gets acquainted to the acrimonious truth—Hyderabad stumbling on in the state of turbulence, turmoil and utter chaos in the Indira Gandhi era. Initially, the lead character feels glad to have procured the rank of a lecturer in a university, teaching creative writing gelled with English poetry—deriving a sense of satisfaction and fulfilment in her life. Howbeit, later when she gets genned-up with the social and political milieu infecting the scene, she begins to interrogate the very need of professing English verses in such country. Mira's conversation with the holy man, Little Mother and her lover, Ramu—accelerates the inner battle for moral code and ethicalness, and existence becomes all the more tangible in a city driven by nefarious and wicked Chief Minister of the state.

A lion's share of the book is set in the holy man's residence. Mira's boyfriend is drawn in the Leftist tussle against an autocratic CM, Limca Gowda, during the Emergency in the Indira Gandhi regime. Margaret Thatcher too gives her glimpse in the novel, conveying a significant message that a mere transmission of political power to a few women doesn't serve as a substitute for women empowerment in a malicious male-structured society. Apparently, the most rebellious step in the novel is that of setting a police station on fire by the crowd in quick response to serene labour-union protests and then a swift reaction for thrashing and raping the captive, Rameeza Be followed by the gruesome act where her husband is put to death. Even the Chief Minister's VIP pavilion and upright cardboard city has been lit to fire. Mira remains baffled, horror-struck and agonized when she catches a glimpse of the rape-survivor, Rameeza Be, first in the blowing police station and then in the 'safe house'. This work of fiction therefore, vibrantly delineates a picture of modern India and the primary character's endeavours to put together her times of yore as she observes the blood-spattered outcome of civil disorder. She strives to reconstruct her own 'self' as well as her traditions and beliefs "the old world is blowing up in our faces" (*Nampally Road*, 33). In this way, Alexander's debut novel is a step towards forceful social writing about contemporary era, from the standpoint of a multicultural woman, who is exiled by her own self.

Reflecting her own experience in the garb of her lead character, Mira, the novelist endeavours to grant a picture of a foreign-returned scholar to the civic scuffle at top gear. The issues brought forth in this piece of fiction are a crisscross of political and social affairs depicted from a feminist lens. The heroine perceives her 'self' split between the political filthiness of the city and her boyfriend, Ramu, Little Mother, Rameeza Be, the victim of police gang rape, a tyrannical and horrific scene of India in the present-day. The chief character of *Nampally Road* exemplifies the fact that even modern woman is required to take an expedition for the purpose of acquiring a sense of identity and meaning in life. The voyage undertaken by women in Hindu Holy Scriptures such as Sita of *Ramayana* and Draupadi of *Mahabharata*, still paces in the contemporary India. The stature of woman has not changed, it is still the same.

In this debut novel, the gamut of female characters is striking, which encompasses a writer, who professes, a labour-activist and a Muslim woman. It connotes a setting demonstrating Indian women under one's thumb alongside freewheeling American women. In fact, *Nampally Road* seems to be an image of India in the era of Indira Gandhi, entwined with the bewilderment of upheaval on the basis of gender as well as class in the country. It is a problem that prevails across different sections of the society. It concerns those who have gained from sovereignty and those whose oppression continues at the hands of the crème de la crème. The book is a true depiction of a woman deprived of political rights, who has been raped in a police station, which causes riots and social hurly-burly. This instance is not just about the heinous crime of raping a woman, but a rape of the powerless by those in power.

Women on this earth, experience numerous refractions. On one hand, she is tyrannized and suppressed, and on the other hand, she is adored as a mother, caretaker, soother, selfless person, who resigns oneself for the family. Woman has always been graded from a male's prospect. Through the recorded past, her place has been hunched by her servitude in the institution of marriage and motherhood.

"Strip it/ block it with blood/ the pages not enough/ unless the sun rises in it..../ I am torn by light/ She cries in her own head" (*FL*, 193). These words bear profound resemblance with Mira's quest, which is not just to 'fit in' in relevance to a place but a universal search for meaning in life, on her arrival to the city of Hyderabad and her political awakening and social roll out in India. She comes to the country with an urge:

> I returned to India determined to start afresh, make up a Self that had some community with what I was. It was my fond hope that by writing a few poems, or a few prose Pieces, I could start to stitch it all together: my birth in India a few years after national independence, my colonial education, my rebellion against arranged marriage, my mother had in mind for me, my years of research in England. How grotesque I had felt, how cramped and small, tucking myself day after into a library seat, reading up on my chosen authors. Now in Hyderabad I was fully adult, in any case my mind had grown stronger. I could live my life. (*Nampally Road*, 30-31)

This internal uproar becomes the external plot of the narrative, in which the author triumphs in brilliantly interconnecting the protagonist's unrest in mind with the civic tussle in the city, by dextrous use of braiding method.

Undeniably, the main character mirrors Alexander's hunt for her identity. The tranquil and protected world of the protagonist at the university is smashed to smithereens by the nonsensical brutality. She tries to connect everything—the moments she lived in England and her willingness to profess in the university at Hyderabad, her liaisons with Durgabai, her affection for writing and her fondness for the love of her life, Ramu. Her experience of such rage, fury, brutality and ferocity in her vicinity taints her idealism. Initially, the grief-stricken protagonist of the novel seeks Durgabai's company for emotional shelter, but later turns to her again, in order to absorb this bitter encounter:

> Listening to her, I lost bitter sense I often had of being evicted, of being thrust out of place in which lives had flat and sharp and broken into pieces. There was tear gas in the present and a woman's terrible cry still hovering over a burnt out police station. (*Nampally Road*, 69)

Eventually, it is through an exploration of her ability to evict, she is able to acknowledge her identity—as an Indian woman feminist.

Thus, in *Nampally Road*, the author makes an earnest attempt to redefine her identity through her lead woman character, which turns out to be an effective means, often acting as an outlet for the author to articulate her anguish. The knowledge of being cut from the mainstream, and the sense of being uprooted several times is what that has been put to light in the novel in the apparel of civic disturbance.

REFERENCES

Alexander, Meena. *Fault Lines*. New Delhi: Penguin Books, 1993. Print.

———. *Nampally Road: A Novel*. San Francisco: Mercury House, 1991. Print.

———. Foreword. *Nampally Road*. By Githa Harihara. Chennai: Orient Black Swan, 2013. Print.

Beauvoir, Simone de. *The Second Sex*. Ed. H.H. Parshley. New York: Vintage, 1989. Print.

King, Bruce. *Modern Indian Poetry in English*. New Delhi: OUP, 2001. Print.

* Co-writer of this essay is Neha Motwani, Asstt. Professor, English, Deptt. of Applied Physics, S.G.S.I.T.S., Indore.

15

Emerging Indian Urban Youth in the Novels of Chetan Bhagat

Chetan Bhagat's novels deal with the aspirations and ambitions, motivations and manipulations, struggles and strategies of survival, compromises and confusions and a questionable and controversial value system of youth. His youngsters are products of post-liberalisation where success is the only mantra; the catch lies in their attempt to save their best years from the drudgery of hard work success entails. His characters want to 'live' and 'achieve' at the same time and find the whole task quite overwhelming. Bhagat tries to capture their ethos in a convincing manner. Their struggle to carve a career and their fallibility has a ring of veracity that strikes a chord with the young reader. To read Chetan Bhagat is to meet a whole urban young world of contemporary India which is grappling with the pressures of cut-throat competition, the stress of the expectations of parents in particular and society in general, the compelling machinations in a manipulative atmosphere and the biological urges and instincts that constantly make them stretch the morality code.

The post-liberalisation scenario in urban India is remarkable not only for the widespread consumerism, it has also witnessed a paradigm shift in terms of cultural environment. Middle-class segment is largely affected by these changes. Boys and girls in their twenties are earning more than their parents; they are going and living abroad or in metros, every middle-class family has a dream that its son or daughter makes it to the premier institutions like IIT and IIM. Young girls have won freedom unimaginable two decades ago. T.V. channels with all their 'beeps' and 'blurrings' are giving a jolt to our sensibility and coming out with shows and serials which shock and tantalise our youth everyday. A product of this globalization and its askewed value system, the youth in Chetan Bhagat's novels is torn between forces that pull it in different directions simultaneously. The psycho-sociological pressures keep interfering with their natural youthful dispositions and alter them at times drastically. Bhagat touches the question related to the sense of responsibility, commitment, apathy, self-esteem, inferiority complex, originality, escapism and the need to think and do things differently for the youth. In *Five Point Someone,* he calls into question the education system that discourages original thinking and research in favour of mugging and getting high grades. Hari, Ryan and Alok try to circumvent this system but ultimately they have to come to terms with it. HOD Cherian's son commits suicide because he cannot live up to the high expectations of his father to get into IIT. In *Three Mistakes of My Life,* Ishan who is involved in sports-coaching tells his friends: "These kids, Govind; Look at them, thirteen-year-old holding their bats with pride. Or the way they want to learn to bowl better. They have a fire in their eyes before every match at Nana Park. When India wins, they dance...of course in two years time they will reach class X. Their bats will be replaced with physics books. And then the spark will begin to die. Soon, they will turn into depressed adults."[1] It is an education system that bulldozes everything. Bhagat does not stop here. He goes a step further and exposes the glamorous and over glorified careers and provides us with an inside view. He shatters many myths. In *Five Point Someone*, Ryan says:

> And this IIT system is nothing but a mice race. It is not a rat race, mind you, as rats sound somewhat shrewd and clever. So it is not about that. It is about mindlessly running a race for four years, in every class, every assignment and every test. It is a race where profs judge you every ten steps, with a GPA stamped on you every semester. Profs who have no idea what science and learning are about. Yes, that is what I think of the profs. I mean, what have

> IIT's given to this country? Name one invention in the last three decades.[2]

He further says, "...this system is an unfair race. If you are a mouse who thinks or pauses to make friends with other runners, or stops to figure out what you want to do in life, or drag baggage from the past...then you will be pushed behind" (101). In his novel *2 States—The Story of My Marriage,* he again exposes IIM education: "We cajoled Ms. Shreenivas for five minutes. I threw in a lot of MBA terms like strategic advantage, bottom line vs. top line, top down vs. bottom up and it made me sound very intelligent. Ms. Shreenivas and Sri nodded at whatever I said. Ultimately, Ms. Shreenivas agreed to nibble at the toxic waste."[3] When these stocks go down seventy per cent and she reprimands Krish for recommending them, he says: "Actually madam, the market went into self-correction mode.... I now understood the purpose of complex research terms. They deflect uncomfortable questions that have no answers" (110). He further observes: "Corporate types love to pretend their life is exciting. The whispers, fist-pumping and animated hand gestures are all designed to lift our job description from what it really is—that of an over paid clerk" (113).

In a fiercely competitive world, Bhagat's characters strive for success. Here the world is sharply divided between 'winners' and 'losers'. 'Looser' is almost an expletive in this lexicon. In order to win, they resort to compromises and bargains which sometimes are far from being ethical or moral. In *2 States,* Krish is a go-getter who makes a deal with his boss for greater leeway in his arrival and departure times in return of his accepting the blame for the latter's inefficiency. It is not only sheer hard work, but also his clever machinations which finally bring his south Indian in-laws round and they accept the Punjabi boy as their son-in-law. In *One Night @ the Call Centre,* Esha pays a heavy price for her dream to be a model when she is physically exploited. She finally realizes, "Any career that makes you compromise on your morals, or judges you because you are not an inch taller is not worth it."[4] In *Five Point Someone,* Ryan, Alok and Hari devise C2D, i.e. Cooperate to Dominate plan which involves copying and save plenty of time for them to have fun. Desperate to get better grades, they even break into HOD Cherian's chamber to steal exam question paper, which proves out to be complete misadventure. Bhagat's youngsters often succumb to the temptations of short cuts and they learn their lesson the hard way. Their dilemma lies in their ambition to carve a successful career and a desire to have unrestricted fun; they are lured by the promises of a market economy on one hand and striving to save their best years from the galley-slavery of the so-called lucrative careers on the other. This is also to be noted that the emerging urban youth is shocked and fascinated at the same time by its growing permissiveness. There are hardly any guilt feelings about its various aspects. The large, lusty and loving youth is shown here with its full force, fascination and fire.

Generation-clash or parent-youth conflict is a significant feature in Bhagat's novels. Ryan and Alok in *Five Point Someone,* Ishan in *Three Mistakes of My Life,* Krish in *2 States*—all have uneasy or troubled relationships with their parents. As Oscar Wilde rightly says, "Children begin by loving their parents, as they grow older, they judge them; sometimes they forgive them." These troubled parent-youth relationships mirror the conflict between the typical Indian family setup with its traditional roles and responsibilities and a global youth culture which is increasingly becoming individualistic and places the call of hedonism and hormones before 'value' and 'morality'. Here is a piece of conversation between Govind and Vidya in *Three Mistakes*: "Passion versus parents is a tough call. But if you have to choose, passion should win. Humanity wouldn't have progressed if people listened to their parents all the time" (103).

But there is also the other side of this fun-loving, liberal, career-oriented and go-getter kind of youth. Bhagat also touches upon the streak of self-destruction in his youngsters. Their frustrations and failures often lead them to suicidal attempts. It is also a known fact that most of the suicide cases take place between the 12 and 25 years of age. In *Five Point Someone*, it is Alok who jumps from the top of IIT building, in *One Night @ the Call Centre,* Radhika takes an overdose of anti-depressants, in *2 States,* Krish has to see a psychiatrist who saves him from a nervous breakdown.

Perhaps it is Vroom in *One Night @ the Call Centre* who voices the youth of today:

> ...and then big companies come and convince us with their advertising to value crap we don't need, do jobs we have so that we can buy stuff-junk food, coloured fizzy water, credit cards and overpriced shoes. They call it a youth culture. Is this what they think youth is about? Two generations ago, the youth got this country free. Now that was something meaningful. But what happened after that? We have just been reduced to a high-spending demographic. The only youth power they care about is our spending power...meanwhile bad bosses and stupid Americans suck the life blood out of our country's most productive generation...." (253-54)

Bhagat's young characters have it all—dreams, desires and daring. Sometimes they are not able to define their dreams and desires and the daring they show is misguided; but the good sense ultimately prevails. In *3 Mistakes of My Life,* he touches upon the political exploitation of youth also. Through Ishan, he records the frustration of the youth of our times:

> The young generation from the Sixties to the Eighties is the worst India ever had. These thirty years are an embarrassment for India.... We played good cricket but that's about it. We remained poor, kept fighting wars, electing the same control freaks who did nothing for the country. People's dream job was government job, yuck, nobody took risks or stuck their neck out. Just one corrupt banana republic marketed by the leaders as their new socialist, intellectual nation. Tanks and thinktanks, nothing else...the clueless Sixties to Eighties generation is now old, and running the country. But the Nineties and the...Zeroes think different but we are being run by old fogeys who never did anything worthwhile in their prime time. The Doordarshan generation is running the Star T.V. generation. (74-75)

Bhagat's forte is his youthful idiom which connects him so well with his young readers. His language is the language actually spoken by the youngsters; it is full of slang, catchy one-liners and is very easy to read—and it is one of the key factors of his overwhelming popularity. Bhagat's use of language is not like that of an established literary writer, but this is precisely what separates him from others. It seems that with Bhagat, Indian writing in English enters into the post-modern phase: it ceases to be literary in the conventional sense and grants easy accessibility to the reader. There is a youthful disrespect to rules in his language. He tries to write from the standpoint of the collective youth and not as a standout on the slanted literary field. In this age of lost innocence, Bhagat's characters also avoid mincing matters and employ a straightforward language laced with colloquialisms, slangs, nicknames and abbreviations. It is a generation using SMS and e-mail language and does not have time to write or read 'between the lines'. So whatever is there, it is open, transparent, lucid and accessible without much effort. There is a certain playfulness and use of humour which again redeem his novels, where situations sometimes become a shade too concocted. Humour also makes him refrain from indulging in sentimentality and keeps his tales firmly on track. Here is an example: "She placed her hand over my arm and self-respecting nitwit that I am, I melted faster than the ice-cream; like the bad mood bugs running through me suddenly got Bagon-sprayed" (*Five Point Someone*, 68).

Bhagat's novels are, without pride or shame, entertainers, but entertainment is not their sole objective—they try to offer a number of self-help tips to their young readers. From this viewpoint, we can even deduce that Bhagat is carving an altogether a new genre in fiction writing—his books are a mix of entertainment, message, romance, smart turns of phrases and humour, which endear them to readers. Bhagat is addressing the youth of his times and he is successful in getting his message across. He might not be a writer of classical fiction and it is quite possible that his writing won't stand the taste of time but then who actually knows about it?

NOTES

1. Chetan Bhagat, *The 3 Mistakes of My Life—A Story about Business, Cricket and Religion,* New Delhi: Rupa and Co., 2008, p. 30. Subsequent references to this book have been incorporated in the text itself after quotes.
2. Chetan Bhagat, *Five Point Someone—What Not to do at IIT,* New Delhi: Rupa and Co., 2004, p. 101. Subsequent references to this book have been incorporated in the text itself after quotes.
3. Chetan Bhagat, *2 States—The Story of My Marriage*, New Delhi: Rupa and Co., 2009, pp. 85-86. Subsequent references to this book have been incorporated in the text itself after quotes.
4. Chetan Bhagat, *One Night @ the Call Center*, New Delhi: Rupa and Co., 2005, p. 230. Subsequent references to this book have been incorporated in the text itself after quotes.

16

Spouse as Stranger in *A Doll's House*

Henrik Ibsen's *A Doll's House* is a play of realization. This realization operates on multiple levels. Nora realizes the patriarchal trap that reduces her in a decorative doll; a 'sparrow', a 'squirrel'—for the amusement of her husband. She realizes that this doll's house is built on her subservient, self-effacing, even self-degrading role of a dumb, beautiful wife and dutiful mother. She realizes that she is made to do a role-play divorced from reality that has deceived her into believing it to be true. She realizes the flaws in the over-protective upbringing of herself from her father. It also dawns on her that it is not the intention but the way in which it is carried out that comes into stringent probe of society. She tries to fit in the persona prescribed for her by society and realizes the futility of such an endeavour. Her embracing of her true self, defying the cocoon in which she was incarcerated is one of the most glorious moments for women in world literature. The slammed door has given rise to much critical censure and speculation but Ibsen here is carving a really new woman—unshackled, unfettered, liberated in the true sense of the term. Even the familial 'obligations' (which are perhaps solely attributed to women) have lost their power to drag her back to the cozy, comfortable and traditional role of a house-keeper, humoring the bread-winner of the family, nursing children, entertaining guests, keeping the appearance of a happy family in the societal gaze, muting her voice, obliterating her identity, trying with all her might to fit in, ever conscious and under constant threat to incur the disapproval of her husband in particular and society in general. She might not find the future agreeable but this plunging into an uncertain tomorrow might be a key to a new, glorious dawn of self-discovery. Ibsen's Nora does what a real housewife ever-concerned for the well-being of her children and family might just fall short of doing—slamming the door on a society which is hell-bent on smothering and suffocating her individuality, which never recognizes her worth and treats her like a doormat so much so that she forgets herself as an entity in herself and is relegated to being just a cog in the gigantic, inhuman social wheel. One of the reasons why Nora retains this abiding appeal as an unforgettable woman character lies in the fearful realization of the consequences and implications of such a drastic step on a social structure which is unabashedly founded on the unsung, unrealized, thankless innumerable sacrifices assigned to women. Nora throws this conditioning and tutoring of society to winds, shaking it to its very unjust and unfair foundations. Hard to emulate, Nora earns our admiration forever for doing what is not done generally.

The most fascinating aspect of the play, however, is the realization of the couple—Nora and Helmer—that they are strangers to each other. Helmer hardly has any inkling of Nora beneath her child-like, prankster, vivacious, bungling exterior for which he feels and acts protective. A benevolent dictator, he smugly controls, directs, dictates, pampers and instructs his wife and is very content playing this. He has no clues to the enterprise of his wife who can be so caring and concerned about his health that she can run the risk of arranging a loan and has the temerity to go to the extent of committing forgery to get what she wants. Always seen as an immature girl, incapable of deciding for herself and in Helmer's view, always in need of guidance, here he finds his wife taking independent decisions, successfully keeping them secret from him, taking bold though wrong steps. This is not the same Nora he knew all along. Similarly, Nora hardly knows the real Helmer until the end beneath the façade of a caring and doting husband. Caged in his convenient idealism, Helmer is more concerned about his social image and appearance in the eyes of people. Instead of realizing the trauma and suffering of his wife which she has undergone for his sake, he sermonizes and acts judgmental. He evinces lack of maturity in handling the uncomfortable ways of Krogstad. By and large goody-goody, Helmer ironically betrays himself as more immature than apparently raw Nora. His shifty ways and changing stands in the wake of changing situations expose the cracks in his integrity. Helmer, in a way, is an epitome of all those males who are quite comfortable with the role of protective, pampering, condescending husbands and to enjoy playing this they need their wives to look up to them for constant guidance and supercilious instructions. Here is a testimony:

Helmer (*standing at the open door*): Yes, do. Try and calm yourself, and make your mind easy again, my frightened little singing-bird. Be at rest, and feel secure; I have broad wings to shelter you under (*Walks up and down by the door.*). How warm and cosy our home is, Nora. Here is shelter for you; here I will protect you like a hunted dove that I have saved from a hawk's claws; I will bring peace to your poor beating heart. It will come, little by little, Nora, believe me (Act III).

It is at this moment that Nora clearly realizes that she has been living with a person whom she has never known. His inability to stand by her in her hour of need reveals his real face and Nora finds herself face to face with a stranger. The play reaches at a point where both husband and wife are revelations to each other; when the marriage crumbles like a ton of bricks; laying bare the lie they were living as their conjugal life. She says:

> Maybe. But you neither think nor talk like the man I could bind myself to. As soon as your fear was over—and it was not fear for what threatened me, but for what might happen to you—when the whole thing was past, as far as you were concerned it was exactly as if nothing at all had happened. Exactly as before, I was your little skylark, your doll, which you would in future treat with doubly gentle care, because it was so brittle and fragile. (*Getting up.*) Torvald—it was then it dawned upon me that for eight years I had been living here with a strange man, and had borne him three children—. Oh! I can't bear to think of it! I could tear myself into little bits! (Act III)

Nora's decision to step out of a false relation is hard to digest for us because we live in a social ambience where hypocrisy happily passes in the name of mutual love and understanding. The play deals a big jolt to the unjust double standards, hollowness of patriarchy and the blind male chauvinism that is impervious to reason and understanding. The play poignantly attains a climax where the years of marriage simply cannot erase the fact that the couple lives like strangers under the same roof until this sordid fact, which is conveniently overlooked by the man and which is insufferable for the woman, stares in their faces. It takes a Nora, brilliantly conceived and portrayed by Ibsen, to make the uneasy choice to opt out of this sham called marriage.

REFERENCE

A Doll's House, Ibsen, Henrik, ebooks@Adilaide, 17 Dec. 2014, Web.

17

The Play as Memory: Tennessee Williams's *The Glass Menagerie*

The Glass Menagerie is a play crafted through the memory of its protagonist Tom Wingfield. At the very outset, the playwright says:

> The scene is memory and is therefore non-realistic. Memory takes a lot of poetic licence. It omits some details; others are exaggerated, according to the emotional value of the articles it touches, for memory is seated predominantly in the heart.

Memory tends to be selective. It preserves what is pleasant and chooses to delete or ignore the distasteful. However, Tennessee Williams doesn't allow Tom to edit out the unwelcome reminiscences. There is no attempt, not even a feeble one, on his part to offer self-justification or apology for what he does in the course of the play. For a memory-play of this nature William's choice of Tom as narrator stands justified. Amanda, with her wishful imagination and with her propensity to give in to the perennial overlapping of her dreams and reality; would have made a mess of this job. Laura, firmly ensconced in her shell, ever jittery to peep out of it, a constant refugee in her quivering reveries and fragile glass animal collection would have been an equally unsuitable narrator. Jim—a brief visitor to this sorry spectacle of half-baked and half-broken, dysfunctional edifice of the Wingfield family would have been even a more inapt choice as narrator. He is the ironically assumed savior who himself is seeking salvation somewhere else. His buoyancy and youthful charm are like the rays briefly illuminating the Wingfield family through the drifting clouds of gloom and hopelessness only to envelope it forever in the unredeemed darkness of despair. Tom's memories are painful, bitter-sweet, ambivalent; their involvement and stoicism both lend an uncanny fabric to weave this play fraught with broken glass unicorns and shattered dreams.

The abode of memory is past. Memories have no future. They take sustenance from the yesterday and fade away in the land of tomorrow. Nebulous, ephemeral, transient, memories do grapple for survival in this predictably lost struggle and yet they are the very stuff this play is made of. Tom Wingfield runs away from them only to re-enter, to re-live. The characters in the play are desperately in search of a tomorrow; wriggling in the clutches of an unrelenting yesterday which is hovering over them, enveloping them like a miasma. Memory is their being. Memory is their nemesis.

Quite significantly, there is the photograph of the absconding father on the wall of the living room, smiling gallantly, ineluctably; "as if to say 'I'll be smiling forever'"[1] (752). Photographs are the things that revive memories. And this one is larger than life size. It is a device to represent the haunting absence of the traditional bread winner, the head of the family, the kingpin who could have kept the family jointed and might have prevented it from falling apart. The senior Wingfield is there, in his blown-up photo hanging on the wall, presiding over this procession of memories, smiling away.

Memories here slide, meld and fuse. But they are far from transforming into nostalgia. Past gets stuck through them. The characters make a desperate attempt to get away and fail miserably. The excruciating torture of memories makes the 'forgetting' impossible. Laura's crippleness has seeped into her psyche. She cannot afford to flirt with hope. Amanda, on the other hand, is seeking comfort in them and we wonder at times whether she fabricates memories, turning them into fantasies. If it is a past that never was—it is all the more painful and if it does have a ring of truth; the pain is even more intense. Her lack of prudence in the matters of heart has cost her dearly. Nevertheless, her adroitness to fashion memories compels her to try to carve a future promising happy memories. This hoping against hope lends her a charm which is both comic and tragic in an undecipherable way. Tom has the courage and will, not strong enough though, to escape yet he cannot be callous enough to forget Laura altogether. He is sick of Amanda because of her loose grip on reality that gets on his nerves; but he is corrupted by a haunting awareness of the utter hopelessness of Laura's situation. It is only just that he is made to narrate the play through his memories; thereby he is made to pay for his attempt to run away from them.

Jim O'Conner is an outsider in the play like a device to set-off the rot of memories eating away into the vitals of the Wingfield family. Ironically, he is himself a memory tucked away in the hidden recesses of an extremely shy girl's mind. The unarticulated crush, the one-sided attention, the fossilized longing—all of it is culminated into a kiss that is soon to become a memory to fall back on. It is the optimum she could receive from her life. Whether Jim will retain any memory of this evening is not difficult to infer keeping in mind his inability to recognize her instantly. Moreover, he doesn't seem to care much. His eyes are glued to the future. He simply does not belong here except in the memory. The memory of an evening in a dark house, feeble lights of candles, trembling shadows on the walls and a trembling girl-pale and wilting; probably would have slipped from his mind, and he will continue to stride ahead treading upon the fallen, dry leaves of the past.

Memory, thus, as employed by Tennessee Williams, is not only a device or technique. It is the very stage of the play. It is *the* protagonist. All the characters in the play define and redefine themselves in its relation. It allows the playwright to leave the things in a blur, in a haze—thus achieving an intended ambiguity. It is the narrator. It is the narration.

NOTE

1. Tennessee, Williams. *The Glass Menagerie*, Pennsbury. 2010. Web. p. 752. Subsequent references to this work have been incorporated in the text itself after quotes.

18

Anne Tyler's *Saint Maybe*: An Epitome of Sibling Compassion and Squabbles

They fight and quarrel,
But soon after they make-up and get amicable.
Arduous to endure each others' glimpse,
But gruesome it is to be without those bickerings.
Keen to pull each others' leg,
Yet stand united in crucial phase.
The longest and most special knot,
Siblings share such exceptional bond.

The 1991 publication, *Saint Maybe* claimed the title of *The New York Times* Notable Book of the year. Undoubtedly, the novel is a remarkable creation from the nib of Anne Tyler, an ingenious author of Southern American literature. The novel is a tapestry exhibiting "the ideal, apple-pie household: two amiable parents, three good-looking children, a dog, a cat, a scattering of goldfish" (Tyler, 4). Primarily, it is an odyssey of the unfathomable guilt embraced by the seventeen-year-old protagonist of the novel, Ian Bedloe, who reckons that his ill-omened words were behind-the-scenes which caused the death of his elder brother, Danny. Commencing this point onwards, *Saint Maybe* becomes the most enchanting and captivating account of the most confusing and puzzling bond of these three siblings, struggling to stand united in such vulnerable phase, where the unfortunate and untimely demise of Danny hurls Lucy into the bottomless abyss of depression—coercing Ian to take charge of the most perplexing, strenuous and backbreaking task of fostering his brother's children—Agatha, Thomas and little Daphne.

Irrefutably, brothers and sisters share the strongest and most fascinating connection on this planet. They are the true gifts of the Almighty, who share the longest liaisons, often outliving the parents. *Saint Maybe* is an archetype of the similar instance.

On and off vigilant and on the ball to the comings and goings in her vicinity, Agatha builds a layer of protection for the later-borns in the narrative, after being orphaned following the death of her mother Lucy. Owing to her sharp and precocious sense and knack of understanding the pulse of moment, she turns out to be acquainted with the fact that her mother "wasn't there behind her face anymore" (Tyler, 58) even months prior to her final departure. In the phase of utter vulnerability and desolate circumstances, the seven-year-old Agatha is compelled to wear the garb of a caretaker to the four-year-old Thomas and the infant Daphne. Nevertheless, no stone is left unturned by Thomas along with her sister, in the guardianship of the youngest sister. The most amusing occurrence of the struggle to put up with the requisites of the notorious Daphne, when a newborn, is brought into spotlight in the following excerpt from the novel, wherein Lucy is taking her afternoon nap and poor baby is wailing to catch up the attention of the elders:

> "Just try her pacifier," Thomas said.
>
> "Well, where'd it go?"
>
> .... "Found it! Thomas crowed. He poked the pacifier between Daphne's lips, but she spat it out again. Her chin began quivering and her eyebrows turned bright pink.
>
> "Phooey," Thomas said. He picked up the pacifier and jammed it in his mouth....
>
> "May be we could feed her in the crib," Agatha said.
>
> ....
>
> Daphne was back to "oho! Oho!"
>
> .... Thomas had his eyes squeezed shut. "Wake up," Agatha told him roughly as she passed. She fitted the bottle between her crib bars and held it toward Daphne. (Tyler, 50-51)

The above illustration confirms the long-standing notion that first-born child has the propensity to guide and pilot the activity and communication of the later-borns. Though both the elder siblings labour in quenching the restlessness of the baby, howbeit it is the oldest one who takes up the cudgels to look after the needs of both—Thomas and Daphne, at the point when the middle child refuses to cope up with the requisites of the bairn and returns to his shell—hurt and not getting along with the unfavourable and not so welcoming manners of Daphne.

Brothers and sisters, who are most affectionate and accommodating, recurrently manifest the most apparent indicators of the sibling rivalry. In fact, "the earliest research on relationships among siblings developed the common theme that brothers and sisters relate to each other mainly in a rivalrous way" (Collins, 87). This notion of sibling hostility received much critical acclaim with theorization of Sigmund Freud, who conceptualized that "this aspect of sibling relationships was a key to subsequent personality differences" (Collins, 87). However, "More recent research...has begun to move away from those polarized views to suggest that rivalry occurs in conjunction with other, separate dimensions of control, conflict, and friendliness" (Collins, 88). The hue of such enmity is reflected in the ties shared by Thomas and Agatha as well, where the oldest sibling every so often explicates the yearning to deliberately hurt the sentiments of her brother Thomas and draw sadistic pleasure and satisfaction from it:

> Thomas forgot three separate times, for instance, three different days in a row, that Danny had gone and died.... "What's the matter with you?" she asked Thomas. "Can't you get it into your head? He had a car crash and he died."
>
> .... Thomas clamped his hands over his ears.
>
> "So when the phone rang we didn't pick it up," Agatha said.
>
> "And when the door banged we didn't unlock it."
>
> Thomas said, "Nee-nee-nee-nee-nee!" but she rode over it....

> She just had these urges to be evil to him. She couldn't say exactly why. (Tyler, 53-54)

Thomas possesses traits of a very sensitive and emotional child, for whom it is too difficult to bury secrets from his closed ones, but Agatha is pragmatic and way too good in concealing things. Thomas naturally spilled the beans and revealed his biological father's identity, Tom Dulsimore, acting as a simpleton to the tactics of Mrs. Jordan. "But all at once Thomas pipes up, 'You're late with the check again, Tom!' he said. Just out of nowhere!" (Tyler, 105). In stark contrast to Thomas, who is dewy-eyed; his sister is smart, brainy and possesses an adult's eye in twigging what's cooking in Bedloes' family, "Hadn't she made Thomas cross his heart and hope to die if he told anyone their mother's things were hidden there? She wouldn't even let him tell Daphne, because Daphne might tell the grown-ups and then the grown-ups would go through their mother's papers and figure out a way to ship Thomas and Agatha off to strangers, keeping Daphne for themselves since Daphne was the only true Bedloe" (Tyler, 138-39).

Daphne being a half-sibling to Agatha and Thomas, was never marginalised or bullied by the other two older siblings, in fact she was showered loved over, cared for and adored in a way which parallels the manner a full-sibling grabs the attention in the family. The reasons for such warmth and geniality in their relation may be possibly due to the untoward loss of Danny, owing to which Lucy grew apathetic in rearing her children. Such circumstances propelled Agatha to assume the role of a mother to 'Daph' at such a tender age. Thomas, being a middle-child simply followed the footsteps of his sister. Consequently, their liaisons deepened and were made firmer with every passing moment.

It is alleged that sibling kinship instantly kick-up a fuss, but a keen observation awakens one to the underlying truth that such grouses and complaints aren't marked by an inherent desire to harm or hurt the other one, but is rather indicative of deep care and love. A touch of bitter-sweet instance which this beautiful bonding assimilates in it is revealed in the following lines of the novel:

> "Have some mashed potato, Honeybunch," Daphne said. She held her spoon out to the little cat, who was sitting on Daphne's lap....
>
> "Ooh, revolting!" Agatha said. "Ian, did you see what she did?"
>
> "What? What'd I do?" Daphne asked.
>
> "You ate from a spoon that cat licked!"
>
> At the end of the table, Thomas gave an elderly cough.
>
> "Well, actually," he said, "the cat's the one who should worry. Mr. Pratt says human spit carries more germs than any other animal's, because humans have these fingers they keep putting in their mouth." (Tyler, 208)

With the threshold of adolescence and embarking towards young age, Thomas grew more poised, the underlying cause for such change might be the interactions with both—Agatha and Daphne—the older and younger sibling. He often seems to incarnate the persona of a peacemaker in the midst of bickering ignited by the two sisters. He transformed into a socially active figure, with the stretch of time, "...he had a whole outside existence—a raft of friends and a girlfriend and an extracurricular schedule so full that he was seldom home for supper" (Tyler, 227).

"As for Daphne, she wound through life sparkling at everyone and lowering her long black lashes over stunning blue-black eyes; but any time you crossed her there was hell to pay. She was fierce, that Daphne" (Tyler, 191). Being a youngest child in the Bedloes, she possesses a happy-go-lucky air, and remarkable gregarious personality. "She dressed like a tiny Gypsy—muddled layers of clothing all tatters and gold thread, purchased on her own at thrift shops—and was generally off in the streets somewhere managing very capably" (Tyler, 227).

A very fascinating occurrence in the work which exemplifies how these three children stand united and shore up the other one is well explicable when Sister Harriet comes to dine at

Bedloes, accompanied by Ian. At this juncture, Daphne through the narration of her dream endeavours to tangential her and guards Ian and other members of the household so that they shun granting more than required attention to Sister Harriet, for she might ruin the siblings' scheme of wanting her uncle to walk down the aisle with Miss Pennington, Daphne's most adored school-teacher. The departure of their guest led to volcanic eruption of Ian's anger over his niece in the swathe of snubbing her. At such onerous point, Agatha and Thomas jumped into the scene to support and at the same time rescue her. "But she [Sister Harriet] wouldn't have taken it personally if grandma had not apologised, Daphne said; and Thomas and Agatha agreed. "She's right," Agatha told Ian. 'It's not Daphne's fault if someone fat was in her dream'.... "Daphne was only making conversation," Thomas told Ian,..." (Tyler, 241).

Studies on sibling relationship concurs the belief that besides 'Birth Order', 'Birth Spacing' is another crucial factor that begets comradeship or enmity in this bond. "Some observers believe that an age gap of two years results in the most conflict between siblings because the older child has difficulty establishing his or her separation from the new sibling.... The teaching role of older siblings also seems to be most effective and positive when they are at least four years older than the younger brother or sister" (Collins, 88-89).

When siblings reach adulthood, it is more likely that they will no longer live in the same place and that they will become involved in jobs, hobbies, and romantic interests that they do not share and therefore cannot use to relate to one another. In this stage, the common struggles of school and being under the strict jurisdiction of parents is dissolved. Despite these factors, siblings often maintain a relationship through adulthood and even old age. Proximity is a large factor in maintaining contact between siblings; those who live closer to one another are more likely to visit each other frequently (Cicirelli).

The amazing companionship which Agatha, Thomas and Daphne shared continued during adulthood, even after the most crucial turning points in their lives, like Agatha's wedlock to

Stuart and Thomas' transformation from American to New Yorkers', attributable to his job at a software company there in New York. This assumption finds its ground during the hours when all the members of the Bedloes assembled prior to the first Thanksgiving which happened to follow the death of Bee Bedloe, their grandmother.

Returning to Baltimore from California, Agatha was the first one to notice the home in absolute turmoil and understand the possible reasons for it, being Bee's death. "I come home and find this place a shambles" (Tyler, 272). As the oldest sibling, she continues to be the person in charge, the route-finder to systematize and standardize things in the household.

> "Tomorrow afternoon we clean house," Agatha told Daphne.
>
> "All right," Daphne said meekly.
>
> "We'll have a regular, normal, home-cooked Thanksgiving dinner; I bought an eighteen pound turkey at the grocery store, and I've invited Mrs. Jordan and the foreigners. Then afterward we'll start cleaning and sorting...."
>
> .... Daphne was so sleepy that the room was misting over, and Thomas had been yawning, but they all settled back obediently and fixed their eyes on screen. (Tyler, 275)

Time plays a very critical and decisive role in life; it puts to test and weights our connections. More often relationships are either crushed or turn topsy-turvy when plonked to such litmus test. However, when roots are strong, and bonds are seeded with deep nourishment of care and fondness, circumstances succumb to take a toll on them. This adage bears its applicability on the attachment of Agatha, Thomas and Daphne, the Bedloes' siblings. Developing in their prime age, in the least diminishes the fragrance of their love and affection, and they continue to squabble, yet stand to advocate, support and hold hands in catastrophic events. Clara Ortega's words truly sum up the essence of this unusual and unparalleled bond shared by these three siblings, "To the outside world we [siblings] grow old. But not to brothers and sisters. We know each other as we always were. We know each other's hearts.... We live outside the touch of time" (Spears 98).

Thus, quite similar to the Bedloe family unit, Anne Tyler's novel *Saint Maybe* is an apple-pie architecture of the extra-ordinary bond of siblings, that evokes a reservoir of as many emotions as generated by the pious tie of parent-child relationship. Nevertheless, the author puts on view her keen observation and dexterity in depiction of this kinship, which takes into its orbit those emotions which are at odds, like a streak of dislike yet a splash of compassion, bequeathing a realistic touch and an effervescent portrayal to these three siblings' characters, Agatha, Thomas and Daphne.

REFERENCES

Cicirelli, V.G. *Helping Elderly Parents: Role of Adult Children*. Boston, MA: Auburn House, 1981. Web. 09 Apr., 2015.

Collins, Lorna et al. *The Modern Family Business: Relationships, Succession and Transition*. Houndmills, Basingstoke, Hampshire: Palgrave Macmillan, 2012 Web. 09 Apr., 2015.

Spears, Lynne. *Through the Storm: A Real Story of Fame and Family in a Tabloid World*. Nashville, TN: Thomas Nelson, 2008. Web. 09 Apr., 2015.

Tyler, Anne. *Saint Maybe*. New York: Random House, 1992. Print.

* The co-writer of this essay is Neha Motwani, Asstt. Professor, English, Deptt. of Applied Physics, S.G.S.I.T.S., Indore.

19

Popular Literature: In the Shadows of Culture Industry

Definitions of culture; and invariably of literature, more often than not are well-embellished hobby horses that are ridden to death. One therefore stands to gain less and lose more by holding streadfastly to a definition that only gives the impression of being permanently convincing. Protracted encounters between thoughts, ideas and sentiments are seen being fleshed out at various sites offered by diverse popular events in literature, music, drama, art as also in society. Literature always compels us to make its definitions flexible enough to accommodate it in the broadest possible terms. Barring a few notable exceptions, literary historians and critics have however, time and again, exhibited a great amount of contempt at the idea of considering popular literature as a subject of serious study. It has been actively ignored and a lot of spleen has been reserved for it. And though it touches us at various levels with so much passion, its persuasions have been denied with more than just a touch of self-vindicating morality. It has been considered a repository of sub-para, and quasi-literature that are less evolved and more corrupting; and it has been accused of a lack of sophistication that is hopeless. 'The powerful legislators of the invisible Republic of letters' believe that culture industry is replacing the authenticity of the regional culture by flat authoritarian—populist versions of a vague universal culture:

> Performativity replaces truth as a goal: truth is manufactured here and now and is sold in retail through the culture-shops. Personalities too are manufactured and exported by

> culture industry.... In the products of the culture industry like pulp fiction, crime thrillers, formula films or television soap-operas, in fact in forms of commercial narrative, everything is expected and known.[1]

Yet it is also a fact that the conceptual category called popular culture affords a generous space where "pitched battles and guerilla wars of the imagination can routinely be seen being fought."[2] One can clearly see that in the criticism against popular literature there is an attitude at work. A kind of classicism that aims at promoting a putative high literature that has met with nods of approval from certain critical quarters. It is necessary therefore to look carefully at the determinants of such an imposed inferiority and try and tease strains that would betray, on the rebound, the definitions of an idealized, academy-ratified 'high literature'.

In this regard, we can very well remember the reception of Shakespeare by the University Wits, the accredited producers of fine literature. Shakespeare "had no theory of literature, only the desire to interest the public, and a talent so flexible that it immediately adopted itself to every *genre* and imitated every note on which a poet had ever played."[3] Shakespeare processed the elements of popular literature in such a way that it suited the untutored taste of the popular audience and the most exacting authentic and ethical standards.

The case of Shakespeare is by no means unique. "Many essentially pop writers have for one reason or another been smuggled into the realm of high art—not by acknowledging the inadequacy of critical 'standards' and adjusting or amending them, but by fudging, lying: hypocritically pretending that works which refuse to die but are woefully deficient in terms of both execution and 'high seriousness' somehow 'do' meet those standards."[4] Mark Twain and Charles Dickens also fall into this category.

II

One realizes only too well that popular culture stands at various level-crossings and is informed by processes like mass-production, canned and uncanned consumerism and merchandised commodification. K. Satchidanandan writes:

> The pressures of the market invite writers to be loud, to follow prescriptions and formulae, to satisfy expectations, to avoid experimentation in form and in content to do away with subtleties and go on repeating what is successful in the market.[5]

There is no denying the fact that popular literature feeds off and into the market economy with missionary relentlessness. But money-making has always been something that evokes ambivalent responses. It was Sigmund Freud who had argued that all artists were driven by fantasies of becoming beloved, famous and rich. George Bernard Shaw is reported to have said to Samuel Goldwyn, "The trouble is that you Mr. Goldwyn think of nothing but art, while all I think of is money." Dr. Samuel Johnson goes to the extent of saying that money is the 'purest' of all motives for writing. Whether successfully or not so successfully, a number of remarkable writers like Scott-FitzGerald wrote best-selling novels and earned a fortune for themselves. Edgar Allan Poe spent his brief career as a back writer and editor of commercial literary journals in pursuit of the common reader and the quick buck. Herman Melville's career also began with the best-seller *Typee*. In fact, those who aspire for critical acclaim and 'an eternal place in libraries' secretly envy and publicly despise the authors of best sellers. It is our fixation with the 'obsolescent myth of the Artist as Victim' that compels us to look at the authors who earn well with the mixed feelings of suspicion and envy. It is an ironical coincidence that Mark Twain fortune was based on the success of *Huckleberry finn* in which the protagonist runs away not only from school, church and family, but money as well, rejecting the treasure which he and Tom had stumbled on at the end of *Tom Sawyer.* "What Twain never wrote was a fictional account of a boy like himself, who...stayed home, grew up,...permitted to be 'civilized' by his wife and daughter, and at last got rich by writing about an eternal child who made all the opposite choices."[6]

Leslie Fiedler finds it hard to confess that,

> Literature, the literary work, remains incomplete until it has passed from the desk to the market place; which is to say, until it has been packaged, huckstered, hyped and sold.[7]

Most of the apostles of High Art who always resent the connection of marketplace and literature are firmly ensconced in the government-funded academies and Bhavans. They are in a position where they can afford to ignore readers and sermonize happily about the perils of popular literature, at the same time using the hard-earned money of the taxpayers who actually constitute the popular readership.

III

The excesses of the high priests of elitism are appalling. They have tried their best to subvert the reputations of the writers who have managed to move both the popular readers and the soft-hearted critics of their own time. Martin Turnell in his *The Classic Moment* dismissed Hugo and Balzac and F.R. Leavis, in his super-elitism, excluded from the 'great tradition' of English fiction, along with Fiedling, Sterne, Scott and the Brontes, the whole *oeuvre* of Dickens. The self-consciously exclusive and self-righteously narrow writers write for a self-congratulatory minority audience which in the name of standards it embodies feels free to ignore books prized by the mass audience. These books include not just Stevenson's *Treasure Island* and *Dr. Jekyll and Mr. Hyde,* but Rider Haggard's *She,* H.G. Wells's *The Time Machine,* and Margaret Mitchell's *Gone with the Wind*; many of which have never been out of print from their date of publication to the present moment. Such popular books live on in the collective memory of us all:

> They are read not for the virtuosity of their authors or the elegance of their structure or style, much less the precision of their language or their subtlety of thought, but for something quite other: their mythic resonance, their archetypal appeal.[8]

There is no doubt that much contemporary critical evaluation regards highly the capacity to disturb and to challenge which is considered to be the prerogative of High Literature, this is nevertheless a limited approach. It fails, for example, to assign much merit to the capacity to delight and to create delight without being trivial is, perhaps, more difficult to achieve. Secondly, this criticism also disregards certain aspects of the expression of individuality and independence through language, its cultural contribution may be significant and lasting. And though it may do so infrequently, popular literature can disturb and challenge. Examples can be cited from the earliest English dramatic literature that has roots in the community, in some ballads and music-hall songs and acts, and even in film and T.V. comedy. When popular art is accepted by critics of High Art, however, it is elevated hierarchically—the works of detective story writers such as Dashiell Hammett in America or Georges Simenon in France are examples in this regard.

A fear of fantasy and a distrust of myth are also responsible for the paranoid reactions against popular literature. What we call 'trash' is rooted like our dreams and nightmares in shared myth and fantasy. It touches us all at a place where we have never been psychically sundered from each other. As for the charge of escapism against it, according to C.S. Lewis, the only people to whom the word 'escape' is a pejorative are jailers. Thoreau observes that 'perennial literature' enables us to be 'in dreams awake', and Freud explains our response to such literature as 'regression in service of the ego.' We seek in popular art a 'privileged insanity', a way of suspending rationality:

> What all popular writers seem to know, including not just Shakespeare and Sophocles, but also Bram Stoker and Edward Rice Burroughs, is that the burden of any system of morality becomes finally irksome even to its most sincere advocates, since it necessarily denies, represses, suffocates certain undying primal impulses which however, outmoded by civilization, need somehow be expressed.[9]

And it is only popular literature that makes this release of the repressed possible, though only symbolically, but the joy and terror we feel are 'real'. Fiedler elaborates:

> Literature which transgresses our taboos teaches us that the impulses of lawlessness preexists in the deep psyches of us all.... Once translated into song and story, however, the released repressed triggers another primeval response; the fear of the unconscious and its tyranny over our bodies as well as our dreams; and by the same token, of the art which simultaneously releases and neutralizes its darker aspects.[10]

It would not be out of place if we take a note of the responses and reactions to popular literature in Hindi. Says Dhananjay Verma, "It is not a mere coincidence that the work which proved to be immensely popular and which compelled readers to learn Hindi language for the promise of sheer enjoyment of reading, was *Chandrakanta* by Devki Nandan Khatri, followed by *Chandrakanta Santati* and then *Bhutnath*."[11] Full of *Aiyari* and *Tilism*, grotesque settings and bizarre happenings, it just swept the readers off their feet. It has attained the status of a classic and as a very popular TV serial, it continues to mint money for its producers. The detective novels of Gopaldas Gahmari were a logical step ahead. Thus, we see that popular literature actually marks the rudimentary stage of Hindi literature and still continues to cast its long and formidable shadow on it. In fact, over the years, in Hindi, popularity is being regarded as a literary crime and if a writer receives cheques of substantial amount as royalty, which is extremely rare, he is banished from the paradise of literature forever. But then, an irresistible leaning towards the popular elements, time and again asserts itself and we find writers like Srilal Shukla who wrote immensely popular *Rag Darbari* trying their hand on mystery in novels like *Adami Ka Jahar* and failing pathetically. He has dedicated this novel to those who have not heard even the names of Kamu and Kafka. This is an ample testimony of the fact that the advocates and practitioners of High Art are also tempted to appropriate a genre that belongs to the realm of popular literature. There may be an implicit desire to address a large number of readers who are blissfully unaware of the existence of these literary giants. We all know about Satyajit Ray's fascination with writing his own kind of eerie stories. He has created characters like Felu Da and Professor Shonku and never disowned them for the approval of highbrow. Ritwik Ghatak, that peerless poet of celluloid, wrote *Madhumati* for Vimal Roy and Khwaja Ahmad Abbas, the staunch leftist, wrote for Raj Kapoor a commercial blockbuster like *Bobby.* Kamleshwar, Dr. Rahi Masoom Reza and Manohar Shyam Joshi belong to that tribe of writers who have churned out popular stuff for films and TV, without losing their eminent positions in the High Art.

In fact, the craving for a story is firmly entrenched in the Indian psyche. *Ramayan* and *Mahabharat* are primarily sources of the gripping and fascinating stories. "Few stories of the world have the story-interest that is aroused by the *Ramayan.*"[12] And as for *Mahabharat,* "The fertility and the richness of imagination shown in the linking of nearly a hundred stories with the central story are breath-taking."[13] This penchant for story explains the popularity of Bengali fiction translated in Hindi. Not only Sarat and Bankim, but their successors like Tarashankar, Shankar, Ashutosh Mukherjee, Vimal Mitra, Asha Purna Devi, and Mahashweta Devi have been immensely popular among Hindi readers, thanks to their skill for spinning riveting tales.

According to the noted Hindi poet and critic, Vishnu Khare:

> If High Arts tend to be snobbish, the common man treats them even more terribly...the apathy of the common reader towards High Art is a result of his resentment and anger. His indifference is not neutral, it is conscious and intended, almost by way of retaliation.[14]

He even goes to the extent of saying that all high language is nothing but 'gibberish' for the common Indian.[15] Three decades ago we had writers who used to find favour with the reading public as well as discerning critics. Amrit Lal Nagar, Yashpal and Bhagwaticharan Verma enjoyed wider readership than any of the present-day novelists. Even today, a work which promises a gripping tale told stylishly, becomes a success. The recent example is that of *Mujhe Chand Chahiye,* a novel by Surendra

Verma which has run into several editions since its publication. It has won Sahitya Academy award and attracted the attention of critics as well as readers. Alka Saravagi's *Kalikatha*: *Via Bypass* also reminds us of the readability of Amrit Lal Nagar and Vimal Mitra, of course with her own stylistic devices in the art of narration.

V

As post-Modernism has collapsed hierarchies like high-brow and low-brow, the number of books is increasingly growing which succeed brilliantly in playful and entertaining mix of the popular and elite fiction. Umberto Eco's *The Name of the Rose,* Paul Auster's *The New York Trilogy* and Arthur Perez Reverte's *The Club Dumas* are notable examples. Donna Tart's *The Secret History* and Peter Hoeg's *Smilla's Sense of Snow* underlines again the masters of High Art are making a sudden foray into popular and succeeding splendidly by bringing something fresh to it.

There are certain broad-based, liberating processes at work even in the so-called culture industry and therefore for all of us, its democratic capacities and its ability to tap and represent the irrational and rational in society makes popular literature an important area of study. It is a shadowland between darkness and light that offers more clues, more insights. There is a need to look at popular literature not disparagingly, but it should be viewed polyangularly and creatively.

NOTES

1. K. Satchidanandan, "Will Literature Survive?", *Indian Literature*, 186, July-August 1998, Vol. XLII, No. 4, 12.
2. Abhay Sardesai, editorial, *Humanscape*, Sept., 1997, Vol. IV, Issue IX, 7.
3. Leguouis-Cazamian, *A History of English Literature*, London: J.M. Dent and Sons Ltd., 1951, 412.
4. Leslie Fiedler, *What was Literature*? New York: Simon & Schuster, Inc., 1984, 123.
5. K. Satchidanandan, "Will Literature Survive?", *Indian Literature*, 186, July-August 1998, Vol. XLII, No. 4, 13.

6. Leslie Fiedler, *What was Literature*? New York: Simon & Schuster, Inc., 1984, 31.
7. *Ibid.*, 24.
8. *Ibid.*, 77.
9. *Ibid.*, 50.
10. *Ibid.*, 42.
11. Dhananjay Verma, "Likhe Ka Rahasya—Romanch", *Nai Dunia*, 29 July 1990, 5, trans. mine.
12. Raghupati Sahai Firaq, *A Garden of Essays*, ed. Dr. Mangal Murty, Patna: Bharati Bhavan, rev. ed. 1989, rep. 1991, 174.
13. *Ibid.*, 175.
14. Vishnu Khare, *Alochana Ki Pahali Kitab*, New Delhi: National Publishing House, 1983, 3, trans. mine.
15. *Idem.*

20

Trials and Travails of Translation

Though translation, as I.A. Richards rightly puts it, is one of the 'most complex activities in the cosmos', we are indebted to it as it bridges the gap between diverse cultures and brings them together. It is only through translation that we get an adequate exposure of the various treatments given to the craft of writing across the globe. A translator smuggles ambience and ethos across the cultural borders. The act of translation, especially literary translation defies a comprehensive general theory and therefore the attempt to theorize it goes on from different angles. But here, we will limit ourselves to the fascination and frustration of literary translation. How does one translate and for whom? How does one choose a text and with what purpose? Such question inevitably lead us to the fact that translation, with its poetics, opens the fresh dimensions of the meaning abounding in critical and interpretative revelations. Newer insights into the text become possible through translation.

Generally, the stigma attached to the concept of translation is that it is not an original activity and that it thrives only in the reflected glory of the original. Indeed, the basic referential material has to be the original piece. But at a deeper level, there is a compulsive need to be authentic to the experience that sought the right expression. The writer too "goes through the process of translation to be able to locate in words the experience of imagination."[1] To translate a story from one language to another does not mean transfer of information. The translated story has to become an experience autonomous and original. The hierarchical relation between the original and the translated then crumbles happily.

The motivation for translation involves a compulsive desire to share the experience of text with someone, even if to cognize it for one's own self. The decoding of the text through mental translation and then its encoding in actual translation in the words of another language calls for tremendous restraint of imagination and responsibility.

A poem or a story is not a riddle to be solved by the translator and even if it is a riddle the reader ought to receive it just the way as the original. The "indeterminacies and multivalances of the original texts need not be sacrificed to make them smooth and readable in compliance with the demands of the market."[2]

The subtle process of some alteration gets inadvertently, but inseparably, infused into the exercise of translation. This does not mean that the original work gets, totally 'lost' in the translation, as Robert Frost believed, or it gets 'demolished' in the translator's endeavour to rationally unravel its mystery as Shelley believed. But certainly there comes into existence a thin lining between the original and the translated one no matter whether the product is better than the original or worse, for, in both cases a departure from the original gets confirmed. This may happen even in the case of a translation done by the original writer himself. And this is not unnatural. When a writer himself translates his work, he may not claim to have recapitulated in totality and exactness the intensity, depth and dimension of the original feeling lived through at the particular moment because two moments cannot be the same nor the reflection of the experience of those moments can be wholly identical.

A translator has to check that his received text does not "over-communicate, paraphrase, expose the under-belly of the creature artfully coiled up in the dark."[3] It is the endeavour of the translator to ensure that "what is personal, specific, idiosyncratic does not become public, accessible and universal."[4] Superimposition of interpretations and theories distance the reader and the relationship to evolve between the reader and the text. There has to be a free mind focused on the experience of the text.

In order to be a transfer of experience and not just a transfer of meaning, translation has to acquire the throb and vitality of life itself. Faithfulness to every letter of the text is in fact likely to create a situation of infidelity to its spirit. Says Dr. Harivansh Rai Bachchan, the famous Hindi poet and translator of major Shakespearean tragedies, "to translate successfully with the same intensity of emotion and experience, if it can be made possible—you have to sink into another medium, another language and come out with all the sound and imagery and associations and rhythms and that one mysterious element which is called incantation, that are essential to articulate the uniqueness of that experience. A good translation, far from just translation, is a transcreation."[5] And it would not be unjust here to add that the *Oxford Advanced Learners Dictionary* explains transcreation standing for "creative translation seen as producing a new version of the original work."[6]

That is exactly what makes a translator a collaborative author, the original text being a focal point of reference. The new language and the owning of the experience by a different mind somewhat alters the text. There is 'equivalence' with a difference and this difference is as creative as the 'original'. The altered text presents its own aesthetics. Equivalence, therefore, is not replication and the original is not replicated. The interesting paradox remains intact: while all literary texts are untranslatable, each one is, in some way, a translation.

Translation has its own validity and exclusive intertextuality. Handling the creative expressions of an experience is a persistent grappling with the nitty-gritty of rejection and selection of words, phrases and structures of sentences. The aesthetic pleasure yielded by the text matches with that of the original. While translating a poem, story or a novel one goes through the same phases—the initial enthusiasm, the inevitable blindness and frustration, and then, the lightening-flash of insights. The intended poem and the poem-in-the making clash, collide, mock and jeer at each other like the source language and the target language.

In Tibetan language, translator has been called, *Lotsava*, one who throws the light. He does not merely translate, he brings the whole concept. To translate is to "make a foray into the consciousness of a language."[7] It is the love for one's authors that makes one choose this form of slavery, this form of freedom. A translator reels from word to word, from image to image, trying his best to articulate the nuances of the source language into the language he can muster, in the rhythm he can produce. Indeed he is a different kind of an author in the act of translation.

NOTES

1. Sukrita Paul Kumar, "The Act of Translation", *Indian Literature*, 179, May-June 1997, Vol. XL, No. 3, 175.
2. H.S. Shivaprakash, "Listen If You Like", *Indian Literature*, 179, May-June 1997, Vol. XL, No. 3, 179.
3. Teji Grover, "A Poet Caged in the Act of Translation", *Indian Literature*, 181, Sept.-Oct. 1997, Vol. XL, No. 5, 131.
4. *Ibid.*
5. Dr. H.R. Bachchan, Pravas ki Dairy, *Bachchan Rachanavali*, New Delhi: Raj Kamal Prakashan, 1984, 411.
6. *Oxford Advanced Learners Dictionary* (First Pub. 1984, 5th Ed. 1996) carries for the first time a supplement which lists and gives the special meaning or usage of over one thousand English words that are used differently in the Indian context. Transcreation is one of these words.
7. Dr. Lokesh Chandra, "Antarjagat ki Yatra Hai Anuvad", *Anuvad*, 87, April-June 1996, 36 (trans. mine).